YOU CAN MAKE IT
How to Obtain and Maintain Freedom From Addictions

Jacqueline Kennedy-Harris

Unless otherwise indicated, all scripture quotations, references and definitions are from the Authorized King James Version © 1987; The New King James Version © 1982 by Thomas Nelson, Inc.; The New International Version 1973, 1978, 1984 by International Bible Society by the Zondervan Corporation; The Amplified Bible Old Testament © 1962, 1964, 1965, 1987 by the Zondervan Corporation; The Amplified New Testament © 1954, 1958, 1987 by the Lockman Foundation; The Message. Copyright © 1993, 1994, 1995, 1996, 2000, 2001, 2002. Used by permission of NavPress Publishing Group. All rights reserved; M.G. Easton M.A., D.D., Illustrated Bible Dictionary, Third Edition, published by Thomas Nelson, 1897; The Name Book © 1982, 1997 by Dorothy Astoria.

YOU CAN MAKE IT
How to Obtain and Maintain
Freedom From Addictions

Jacqueline Kennedy-Harris
jacqwheel@aol.com
(773) 732-5784

Copyright © 2016 Jacqueline Kennedy-Harris
ISBN 978-1-943343-28-7

Published by
PublishAffordably.com | Chicago, Illinois

DEDICATION

Dedicated to all of my family and friends who prayed for and supported me while writing this book.

I would also like to thank the members of my family who were willing to answer questions and share personal information in order to see others set free from addictions.

YOU CAN MAKE IT

INTRODUCTION

Have you ever found yourself in a situation that caused you to feel as though there was no way out of the mess you had gotten yourself in? Hopeless, dreadful, in a dark place, held captive by Satan, the very enemy of your soul, due to thinking you would be able to do something forbidden and be able to stop whenever you got ready to? Questioning yourself, "How did I get here? Am I going to die in this state that I have gotten myself in?" Life is full of choices, and sometimes we just don't make the right ones. We are people, fallible human beings bound to make mistakes in spite of how smart and strong we sometimes think we are. However, mistakes can be corrected.

As you read this book, you are guaranteed to find out when, why, and how you got in the situation that you have found yourself in. You will also learn the steps that you must take in order to get out of the situation. People are racking their brains trying to find solutions to their problems. Scientists are working hard trying to find the cure for different diseases that have crept upon the earth. Using natural devices to solve spiritual problems is only a waste of time. You must solve spiritual problems with spiritual solutions.

Can't you see after all this time you have just been spinning your wheels, and nothing has happened? You have tried everything else that you thought could help you. You have called everybody else who you thought could help you. So did I! I found myself in captivity with a bad drug habit that I just couldn't seem to shake, no matter how hard I tried. My looks were gone; I had lost everything I had, even my integrity. I was in the worst state I had ever been in, in my whole entire life, doing things I thought I would never do, saying things I thought I would never say and going places I thought I would never go.

Then one day I remembered the words of my dear grandmother, who had spent the majority of her life trying to tell me I needed to call on Jesus way before I had ever ended up on drugs. I had been in my situation so long and had messed up so bad, that I was battling in my mind and having thoughts that even Jesus doesn't want me now. Well, what could I lose by trying to call Him anyway? Everything else had failed. The drug rehab couldn't help me, family members couldn't help me, friends couldn't help me and even the men who took interest in me that desperately wanted to help me couldn't help me. Why? I know now. Because I had a spiritual problem that mortal man could not solve.

There I was one night, walking down the street hollering from the top of my lungs, screaming, "HELP ME, JESUS! HELP ME JESUS! HELP ME!" as my salty tears streamed down my dark, ashy cheekbones that had become so thin due to the drug addiction I had ended up with. I was literally suffering from malnutrition because of the dumb decisions I had been making for so long. When I had the opportunity to choose between drugs or a decent meal to eat, I always chose drugs because I was powerless over my situation.

Well, finally Jesus showed up and saved me, just like Grandma said He would.

Be blessed as your life is transformed while thumbing through the pages of my book.

YOU CAN MAKE IT

TABLE OF CONTENTS

-One-

SATAN'S DEVICES

Satan uses a lot of different tactics, weapons and devices in order to carry people into captivity. He has studied each and every one of us since birth. He knows what we like and what we don't like. He knows our strengths and our weaknesses too. He strategically and skillfully chooses the weapons and devices he is going to use on each one of us. His choices of weaponry, devices and temptations are mainly selected by what he thinks we will be weak enough to fall for and skillfully crafted for the type of captivity or sin he is trying to carry us into. The Bible tells us a lot about the devil's skills, strategies, characteristics and tactics so that we will be aware of them. This is why he is called by so many different names in the bible. Names have meanings and are often used to describe a person's personality and characteristics. Names also carry a certain amount of authority. He is referred to as Satan, Lucifer, Apollyon, Abaddon, Belial, Baal, Beelzebub and many more.

Although the Bible warns us about the devil and his devices, it assures us that we have power over all the power of the devil and nothing shall by any means hurt us (Luke 10:19). There is only one true God. He has a lot of names too. He has given His Son Jesus a name above every name, far above all principality, power and might (Ephesians 1:21). And at the name of Jesus every knee shall bow and every tongue shall confess that Jesus Christ is Lord (Philippians 2:10-11). Even as we believe there is one God, the devils also believe and tremble (James 2:19). Jesus promised us if we ask anything in His Name He will do it (John 14:14). God loves us so much that He gave His only begotten Son, Jesus, that whosoever believe in Him should not perish but have everlasting life (John 3:16). The Word of God also assures us that, "No weapon formed against us shall prosper" (Isaiah 54:17).

As I began to look over my life, I began to realize that it was due to generational curses, rebellion, rejection, pride and the curiosity of my own mind that I eventually ended up strung out on drugs. I believe these are the five major spirits, weapons and devices that the devil uses in order to carry people into various types of captivity.

Satan uses demons in order to make us feel certain ways and do certain things. He has one mission in mind: to kill us, steal from us and destroy us. Satan's kingdom is very well organized and he prefers for demons to reside on the inside of us because they have a greater advantage of carrying out his plans. We are all born with demons, unclean spirits, on the inside of us. And it is the devil's intention to fill our lives with more demons, meaning that demons that are not on the inside of us are always trying to find a way to enter in. They are able to enter in through making suggestions that we try certain things and do certain things. When we come into agreement with those suggestions, they have the ability to enter in. In Luke 22:1-6, the bible tells us about how Satan entered into Judas Iscariot one of Jesus' disciples so that he would betray Him. Just think about it, you were not smoking cigarettes, drinking alcohol, using drugs or having sex when you were born. Satan suggested that you try it, when you agreed, he entered in so that he could assist you with doing those things. Now it is hard for you to stop because you need Jesus to set you free. Always remember if you ask anything in Jesus Name He will do it for you.

Our Lord and Savior Jesus Christ came to destroy the works of the devil (1 John 3:8). It is His desire to transform us into His war weapons. In Jeremiah 51:20, God says we are His battle axe and weapons of war. In order to become His weapons of war, we must allow Him to change the way we think, change the way we do things and teach us spiritual warfare. We must understand that we are not fighting against people, we are fighting against demonic spirits that are sent on assignment to invade our lives and make havoc of us in any way that they can. The only way we can prevent the devil from carrying out his will for our lives is by turning our lives completely over to the Lord. We must learn how to strategically pray and study the Word of God. King David said, "Thy Word have I hid in my heart that I may not sin against You" (Psalm 119:11). It is then that we can become more than conquerors through Him who loves us (Romans 8:37). It is then that we receive power over all the power of the enemy. We receive power over generational curses, rebellion, rejection, pride and every demonic spirit that is released by Satan to try to kill us, steal from us, or destroy us.

Generational Curses
Generational curses are curses that are often passed down through our bloodlines from generation to generation due to the disobedience of our forefathers. According to Marilyn Hickey's book *Breaking Generational Curses*, "These curses are unclean iniquities that increase in strength from one generation to the next, affecting the members of that

family and all who come into relationship with that family."
We often think we are going through things because of
something we have done, which is true at times, but this is
not always the case. Some of our lives have been targeted,
due to the iniquities committed by our forefathers.

The wickedness and sins people refuse to deal with in their
lives will sometimes have the opportunity to visit the lives
of their children, grandchildren, great-grandchildren and
even their great-great grandchildren (Exodus 20:5). During
my research, I found out that according to Addictions and
Recovery.org, they even believe that children of addicts are
eight times more likely to develop an addiction. One study
looked at 231 people who were diagnosed with a drug or
alcohol addiction and compared them to 61 people who did
not have an addiction. Then it looked at the first-degree
relatives (parents, siblings, or children) of those people. It
discovered that if a parent had a drug or alcohol addiction,
the child had an eight times greater chance of developing an
addiction. I did not get where I am today by going to a
twelve step program but you must do what works for you.
However, I would advise you to make sure that you make
Jesus your higher power. I only had to take one step instead
of twelve steps. My one step was turning my life over to the
Lord. The demons that had entered into my life were too
strong for me to have the ability to sit in a twelve step
program. I tried but they always ran me up out of those
programs. I needed God. He was the only antidote to my
situation.

In Psalm 51:5, David one of the greatest kings in the bible
that God considered to be a man after His own heart stated
that he was "shapen in iniquity; and in sin did his mother
conceive him." That word *shape* means "to form, train, or
influence someone greatly." The environment that a person

is raised in has the ability to shape and influence them. When people grow up in homes where one or both of their parents are alcoholics and/or drug addicts, they tend to think drinking and drugging are normal.

King David also said, "in sin did his mother conceive him," which means he was stating that he knew that it was either his mother's or father's genes that he received during conception that caused him to be in the spiritual condition that he was in and the reason that he was sinning. David wrote Psalms 51 because as much as he loved God he had fell into sin. He was repenting and pleading with God because one day, he slept with a woman by the name of Bathsheba, who was the wife of Uriah, one of his dedicated soldiers. Bathsheba got pregnant by David through that one act of adultery. In order to cover up his sin, David sent for Uriah and sent him home, to be with his wife with hopes that he would sleep with her so that he would believe that the child she was pregnant with was his own. However, Uriah was so dedicated to David that he refused to go home and sleep with his wife. Instead he chose to sleep at the door of David's house with the rest of the soldiers.

Because King David's plan didn't work, he sent Uriah back to battle and sent a letter to Joab, the captain of his army, and told him to set Uriah in the forefront of the hottest battle so that he would be smitten and killed. The baby that Bathsheba was pregnant with by David died. However, after Uriah was killed by the command of David, David married her and she got pregnant by him with another son by the name of Solomon. Solomon who was apparently fighting the same demons his father David had, ended up with a love for strange women. His love for strange women caused him to begin to serve their foreign gods. Solomon ended up having seven hundred wives and three hundred concubines.

The sin that blossomed in David's life revisited the life of his son Solomon at an even greater degree.

We must deal with sin in its embryo stage because if we don't it will grow and cause us greater problems. Demons will run rampant in our lives if we don't cry out to God for help. James 1:14-15 tells us that every man is tempted when he is drawn away of his own lust and enticed. Then when lust hath conceived, it brings forth sin: and when sin is finished it brings forth death.

Let's look at that word conceive and bring forth for a minute. To conceive means to become pregnant and to bring forth means to give birth to. When we get pregnant with the seed of sin such as alcohol, drugs, lust, perversion, etc., we give birth to a demon that has to be fed. The more we feed it the more it grows and the stronger it becomes. That is why it becomes an addiction. Many of us call it a habit. While in all actuality it is a demon that needs to be cast out.

Satan never gives up. If he is unable to enter into us through our bloodline, he will always try other options because he is an opportunist. An opportunist is a person who exploits circumstances to gain immediate advantage rather than being guided by consistent principles or plans. Don't be deceived; Satan will use every available opportunity he is granted. He will use people in the neighborhood where people grow up in to try to influence (tempt) them, or people they meet at a school, party, or any other events that they attend. He doesn't care who he uses. He just wants the job done. We are not wise if we refuse to turn our lives over to the Lord because He is the only one that can cause us to become wise as serpents and harmless as doves (Matthew 10:16). In Daniel 1:20 the king that was over Babylon found Daniel, Hananiah, Mishael and Azariah ten times wiser and better than all the magicians and astrologers in his whole realm. We need God in our lives in order to have the wisdom and the ability to defeat and outsmart the devil. Without God we can do nothing (John 15:5).

Rebellion
According to the *Webster Dictionary*, rebellion is "open opposition toward a person in authority; a refusal to obey rules or accept normal standards of behavior, dress etc." When we as people refuse to obey the Word of God, we are automatically headed for trouble because it diverts our life off God's course for our life. Jonah's life is a perfect example of how we as people can get off course and waste time. We also encounter some of the things we end up encountering because we choose to walk in open rebellion toward God. The Lord had told Jonah to go to Nineveh and warn the Ninevites about His impending judgment because of their wickedness, but Jonah decided to run from God and paid his fare to go to Tarshish. Tarshish was about as far as you could go in the opposite direction from Nineveh. Some people have been running from God so long they don't even realize how far they have run.

When we run from God it interferes with the relationship we have with him. Jonah was not a sinner he was a prophet of the Lord. We must always examine ourselves to see if we are in the faith (2 Corinthians 13:5). The reason Jonah did not want to warn the Assyrians of their wickedness was because Jonah did not want them to repent and receive God's mercy. It is very important for us to deal with the matters of our hearts because we all have different reasons for rebelling against God. Some people rebel against the Word of God due to greed or lust. Some rebel because of deep hurt and the inability to forgive, while others rebel because of the lust of their flesh. Rebellion is such a strong spirit that the Bible says that rebellion is as the sin of witchcraft and stubbornness is as iniquity and idolatry (1 Samuel 15:23). Spirits of rebellion and stubbornness operate together. Stubbornness fortifies the spirit of rebellion. As we recently stated, rebellion is open opposition toward a person in authority; a refusal to obey rules or accept normal standards of behavior, dress etc. Stubbornness means having or showing a dogged determination not to change one's attitude or position on something, especially in spite of good arguments or reason to do so. In spite of the spirits of rebellion that operate in our lives, whether we are saved or not, God has mercy on us and is always willing to deliver us when we repent.

All rebellion is sin, iniquity, or transgression. Exodus 34:7 says, keeping mercy for thousands, forgiving iniquity and transgression and sin. That word *mercy* means that He does not give us what we should have gotten for the sin, iniquity, or transgression that we have committed. The Scripture also says He will forgive our iniquity, transgression and sin. When you forgive somebody for something, that means you no longer hold that person accountable for what they did. To forgive also means to stop being angry about something; to pardon somebody; cancel the obligation, excuse, absolve, or exonerate. Hebrews 8:12 says, "The Lord will be merciful to our unrighteousness, and our sins and our iniquities will He remember no more."

This exoneration was given to us as part of the New Covenant. Therefore, if the Lord has forgotten about the sins and iniquities we have committed, then we must forgive ourselves for the things we have done in the past, forget about them, and move forward. Let's take a look at what sins, iniquities and transgressions are. To sin means to miss the mark or fall below the mark of what God has called us to do. We have all missed the mark at different times in our lives. We can put an end to sin by repenting and submitting to deliverance. Demons cause us to sin and they must be cast out. The word *iniquity* means to be twisted, bent or distorted. It also implies a certain weakness toward a certain sin. Sin becomes iniquity when you keep committing the same act over and over again until it becomes a perpetual habit. When sin become iniquities, they are passed through the bloodline. What we fail to put an end to in our lives will try to continue on in our children's lives up to the third and fourth generation. To transgress means to trespass or overstep pre-established boundaries. A good example would be when our parents told us not to go certain places and we went anyway, or they told us not to hang out with certain people, but we hung out with them anyway and off into captivity we went. Whenever someone is telling us something for our own good, we should ask God to help us be obedient to him or her. Obedience will save us from a whole lot of troubles, heartaches and pain. Do not play around with sin because you can end up being in bondage much longer than you anticipated.

Rejection
Rejection means to dismiss as inadequate, inappropriate, or not to one's taste; to fail to show due affection or concern for someone; rebuff; a person or thing dismissed as failing to meet standards or satisfy tastes. We have all experienced rejection in our lives. Rejected people desire to be accepted by those who are rejecting them. It is a terrible feeling to feel unwanted. Everybody wants to be liked and accepted by others. Joseph's brothers rejected him because their father favored Joseph and rejected them. Due to the rejection they were experiencing because of Joseph they also ended up being jealous of him. Throughout the entire Bible we see acts of rejection. Rejection causes people to

seek attention and love, sometimes in all the wrong places. Joseph thought that if he told his brothers about his dream of how God was going to raise him up to be in authority, and how they were all going to bow down to him, that they would accept him, but the Bible says they hated him the more. Those dream killers hated Joseph so bad that they not only rejected him, but due to their jealousy they wanted to kill him. The bible tells us that jealousy is as cruel as the grave (Song of Solomon 8:6).

Joseph's brothers threw him in a dark pit where there was no water so that he could possibly starve to death or die of thirst. Jesus's own people rejected Him. Almost every person that God raised up in the Bible who became a powerful person experienced being rejected at some point in their life. The spirit of rejection makes some people make a great name for themselves so that they won't be rejected. Others bow down and do things that they normally wouldn't do in order to be accepted by the group of people they desire to hang out with.

Rejection can either end up making a strong leader out of a person or a gofer, flunky, or follower. In spite of the rejection that Joseph suffered from his brothers, he ended up becoming the governor of Egypt and ended up having to feed them. Matthew 21:42 tells us that the stone which the builders rejected is become the head of the corner. Romans 8:28 tells us that all things work together for good for those that love God and are called according to His purpose.

Pride
The Bible lets us know that pride goes before destruction and a haughty spirit before a fall. When we as people begin to think of ourselves more highly than we ought to think, we are headed for destruction. Pride makes one think they are

stronger than they actually are, smarter than they are, wiser than they are and even look better than they actually do. Pride will make you feel as if you can conquer spirits that others have fallen prey too. We should be confident, not prideful. God hates pride. The only way we can conquer spirits that others fall prey too is by the help of God.

We see how drugs have defeated so many people. But pride will make us feel as though we can try them or pick them up and put them down whenever we get ready to and that they will not have the effect on us as they have had on others. I thought I had everything together when I first started using drugs. I have been able to retrieve some pictures of myself that show how the devil had dogged me out so bad with the spirit of addiction. They would scare you if you saw them. You would not believe I am the same person on those pictures that I am now, since the Lord has cleaned me up and fixed my life.

Curiosity
Adam and Eve had everything they needed when God placed them in the Garden of Eden. God told them not to eat from this one tree, the tree of the knowledge of good and evil. Eve was so curious she could not resist Satan's suggestion of eating from the tree in spite of the fact that God had told Adam that if they ate from the tree they would surely die. Through curiosity some people have tried drugs and it has cost them their very lives due to an overdose or getting killed due to doing something scandalous they did in order to obtain more drugs.

Of course we could write a whole book about each of these spirits and devices that Satan uses to cause us to end up on drugs or fall into some other form of captivity. However, it doesn't matter what weaponry Satan uses, *You Can Make It.*

SKELETONS IN THE CLOSET

While growing up, the majority of our parents tried to keep a lot of things they and other members of our families had done in the past hidden from us. Those secrets only gave the devil the ability to take advantage of us, because many of us were having different types of struggles, temptations and ungodly desires and didn't know why. In addition, if we found out about some of the things they were embarrassed about, we were immediately told, "What goes on in this house stays in this house," in such a harsh way that we were too afraid to tell anybody. As a result of their secrecy, many of us are still struggling with things we probably could have been delivered from years ago. The enemy uses spirits of fear of not being accepted by others, guilt, shame and embarrassment to get us to cover or hide things that we have done in our lives in order to keep us in various types of bondages. In Ezekiel 28:16, the devil is called the covering cherub, which describes another one of his attributes. He loves to cover things up.

The devil needs to be exposed. We should tell somebody about the secret sins that have been hidden and covered in our lives and our family tree for years, decades and probably centuries! I am by no means saying we should tell everybody, but again we should at least tell somebody. We should make sure that the person or people we decide to tell are walking in a certain level of spiritual maturity and authority. They should be someone we can trust, who will pray for us and who loves the Lord and us too much to hurt us by telling other people. Immature people will take the secrets that lie deep in our hearts, which we have entrusted them with, and use them as weapons to beat us over the head with later, especially if we ever get into an altercation with them.

Sometimes due to past hurts and disappointments we end up harboring demons due to feeling as though we could never trust anybody again. Satan uses the lack of trust along with hurts and disappointments to paralyze and cripple us. He knows that if we hold certain things on the inside, we will never have the opportunity to grow, change, get healed, set free, delivered, or transformed because a person who covers their sins will not prosper, grow, or be transformed (Proverbs 28:13). Regardless of the betrayals and disappointments that we may have encountered in the past, there is always someone we can trust, because the Bible tells us to confess our faults one to another and pray so that we can be healed (James 5:6).

God loves us and wants us to be free; therefore, He always forewarns us about the generational curses that will most likely try to operate in our lives because we have already been delivered from the curse of the law. However, our enemy, the devil, will still try to illegally put things on us, especially if we do not know our spiritual rights. Always remember that the devil is a legalist. A legalist is a person who is still operating under the old covenant, which is the law.

Either the Lord will tell us which generational curses are trying to operate in our lives, or He will make one of our ancestors tell us so that we will strategically know how to pray for ourselves. When I was a child there was a lady in my life who knew my mother, grandfather and grandmother very well. We called her Aunt Della, although she was not really related to us. As a child I would spend the night over Aunt Della's house, and she would share things with me about my family that I didn't know. People are even more open now when it comes to telling us things than they were in the past because everybody and everything have come out of the closet. I take advantage of every opportunity that arises for me to find out something about the lineage that I was born in. I would admonish you to do the same. When we ask questions for the right reasons, people will be willing to answer them.

Due to how subtle, deceptive and rebellious the devil is, we must pray daily, binding the generational curses that try to plague our lives. In addition, due to the secrets many of our parents have held back from us, we must keep our communication lines open with God so that He can let us know the areas that the enemy is going to try to attack us in. It would be to our advantage to know every spirit that has operated in our generation, whether through sin or sickness. Life is in the blood. This is why the first question the doctor asks us when we go to the doctor is if there are any sicknesses that our parents or grandparents had that we know about, such as cancers, diabetes, high blood pressure etc. Psychiatrists ask the same questions, because mental illness and addictions can also be inherited.

If we really want to get set free, we are going to have to expose all the skeletons in our closets. In some cases, we must be willing to expose the skeletons in the closets of our ancestors. According to Wiktionary, the free online dictionary, the term "skeletons in our closet" is an idiom used to describe an undisclosed fact about someone, which if revealed, would have a negative impact on the perception of that person; such as literally having harbored corpses or cadavers in the concealed portions of one's abode for a period of time long enough for them to decompose into nothing more than bones. Satan uses spirits of embarrassment and shame in order to keep his captives in captivity as long as he can, or for better words—keep the skeletons in our closets.

One of the most precious spiritual truths that I have learned since I have been in the body of Christ is to be transparent so that I would have the ability to get the help that I needed. In the process of me being transparent, it has also helped so many other people to become transparent so that they could also get the help they needed. There are many embarrassing things that I have experienced in life. Some things I share with everybody, but there are some things I only share with people that I am led to share them with. Immature people are usually very judgmental and critical, while mature people are very compassionate and concerned about the welfare of others.

Due to the fact that we don't know what some people will do with the information that we would share with them about somebody else, we should always allow other people to share things about themselves to those they desire to share them with. We as people will sometimes be willing to share things about other people while hiding, covering and protecting the skeletons that we have allowed to remain in our own closets.

True story: A young lady had gotten pregnant by a close

friend of her family that had raped her decided that she did not want the baby, so she gave the baby to a lady that she knew. When the little girl turned twelve years old, she started acting out with the lady that her mother had given her to, so the lady wanted to give the baby back to her mother. The mother did not want her daughter back. She also had two other children who told their mother that the little girl was not their sister, which encouraged the mother to harden her heart and refuse to accept her daughter.

I told the mother that it was not the child's fault that she was born through her being raped and that she was wrong for rejecting and punishing her daughter because of what happened to her. I also told the mother that she should get her daughter and let her know that she was raped and that she was sorry for rejecting her all those years. Those skeletons that she has been hiding in the closet by not allowing her daughter to know that she gave her away because she was raped are causing her and her daughter to harbor corpses that they can get rid of by exposing them. Those skeletons are also affecting her other children too, because they are too selfish and inconsiderate to be concerned about the pain that their little sister is going through due to being separated from her biological family.

Are you hiding something that is tormenting you and trying to drive you crazy? Are you holding on to secrets that are keeping you from getting set free? Is there a family secret that you have swept up under the rug that is causing your whole family to suffer? Set yourself free and the other members of your family. Learn how to strategically pray and break the curses off of your bloodline.

Father God, I take authority now over every generational curse, every spirit of addiction, every sickness and disease that has plagued the lives of your people and I release your consuming fire to burn out everything that is not like You out of our lives in Jesus name.

God said this is the season that He is getting ready to bring to light the hidden things of darkness. He is opening up the prison doors and He is going to bring His people out of captivity that have been held in captivity due to a lack of knowledge of things that have operated in their bloodlines from generation to generation. He is opening up the blind eyes, and the deaf ears, and He is downloading His instructions and strategies on the inside of us. He is going to raise many of us up to do damage to the kingdom of darkness because there is a holy anger coming upon us that we have never experienced before, and we shall battle against the kingdom of darkness, and we shall prevail. And God shall restore the years that the cankerworm, the palmerworm, and the caterpillar have eaten up. And we shall enter into our Promised Lands because the ability to break through every obstacle is coming upon us in an unusual way. And we shall be a victorious people in the land.

Two

MY STORY

My Origin

My mother is eighty-two years old, while I am writing this book. And I have the ability to call her from time to time to ask her lots of questions so that I can get a clearer picture of how and why certain spirits that have operated in our family tree had the opportunity to visit my life. The transparency of my life and the lives of my family members that are written in this book are only written because I have a strong desire to assist people with getting set free from the generational spirits that are possibly running rampant in their families.

My mother was born and raised in St. Louis, Missouri, but once she got old enough, she moved to Chicago with her aunt Margaret, my grandmother's sister. While living in Chicago my mother met my father, a veteran who had fought in the Korean War who was a tall, city-slick, slender handsome man. My parents were not married, so my oldest sister and I, who my mother had by my father, were born out of wedlock.

Although I was born in Chicago, I was raised in St. Louis, Missouri, for twenty of the first twenty-two years of my life, because when I was only two years old, my mother relocated from Chicago back to St. Louis. I was told by my mother that she moved back to St. Louis from Chicago because my father had beaten her so bad that we would not have recognized who she was. All I can say is that when my mother left my father with my older sister and me, she had the strength to leave and never look back.

My mother also told me, one day, she had seen with her own eyes my father almost brutally beat a man to death because his money had come up missing out of his pants pocket. The man that my father assaulted was renting a room from my father at the apartment that he and my mother were residing in at the time.

While growing up in St. Louis, my mother never tried to keep me and my older sister from knowing our father, so we were allowed to visit him here in Chicago several times. While visiting my father, he and the lady that later ended up being his wife and our stepmother were only living together. During our visits, my father never spent any valuable time with us; we were left under the care of our stepmother. My stepmother has also been very instrumental in assisting me with writing this book. While writing this book and asking questions, my stepmother told me that everybody on my father's side of the family were fighters and very hot-tempered. She also told me that my father had been to jail for stealing from the railroad when he was working for them. And he had to spend about six months in jail before they were able to get him out.

My father was a gambler; he would often play blackjack, poker, and shot-loaded dice all night long. One night he got mad and shot a man because he had won all the money, but the man was afraid to go to court in order to press charges against him. She also told me that my father used to pimp women. My father's baby sister died at the age of thirty-seven because her organs shut down due to drug abuse. She was an intravenous drug addict and a prostitute.

I need you to pay close attention to the things that I am writing in this book, because the reason I am mentioning the spirits that have operated in my ancestors lives is because they have also operated in my life, some on a greater level.

As I previously stated, according to my mother, when she left my father, I was two years old and my big sister was three. I also know that I have some Indian blood from my father's side of the family. I have often heard that most Indians are mean by nature. I also have some Jewish blood in me from my mother's side of the family because my mother's grandfather on her father's side was a Jew. I never met my Jewish grandfather because he died before I was born.

My father was a veteran, which means he had to fight in the war. I am sure he had to kill many people as well as see a lot of people get killed. My father would have bad dreams. He would often wake up fighting and saying the dogs were chasing him. My father told me out of his own mouth when he was in the war the Koreans would put bombs on innocent babies and when the soldiers would pick the babies up they would get blown up. My father also owned a couple of taverns in Chicago, which he allowed me to work in one when I was only sixteen years old. I was visiting during that time; I was not officially living in Chicago yet. My stepmother said everything my daddy did was crooked. She also told me that my father used to snort cocaine, smoke marijuana and I know for a fact, he loved drinking his beer.

I also discovered that I had another brother and sister that my father had by another woman. My sister by the other woman and my sister by my mother are only days apart in age. My half-sister and half-brother had the opportunity to know things about our father that I would not have known, because they were raised up here in Chicago. They also used to live with our father during certain periods of their lives. I later found out a lot of things about my father through my half-sister that I don't feel the liberty to share at this time. However, I thank God for letting everyone who has shared things with me share them, so that I would know how to pray against the generational spirits that have already attacked my bloodline, as well as those that could possibly try to attack my bloodline in the future.

So now we know that on my father's side alone, we have spirits of anger, fighting, violence, murder, torment, spirits of whoredom, cheating, fornication, pimping, lawlessness, lying, stealing, gambling, alcoholism and drugs. I can honestly say I have seen each one of these spirits operate in my life, except the spirit of murder.

My father was a very handsome man, the playboy type, and he and the women in his life only lived together. He did eventually marry my stepmother after shacking up with her for over nineteen years. She didn't have any biological children by my father, but she already had a daughter when she met him, who ended up being my stepsister. My stepmother told me that she was twenty-seven years old when she met my father and he was thirty-nine years old. He was a little over twelve years older than she was. And as old as my father was before he died, he still had a young girlfriend on the side. My father was sixty-seven years old when he passed.

There is not a whole lot that I know about my mother's flaws, because I lived with her and there are some things a parent would never tell their children. However, I do know that although my mother was never married to my father, she was only married once. She married my little sister's father, but that marriage did not last long. She later started going with another man and had a son by him, who is my little brother. Therefore, my mother had four children. Two of us were by the same man, who was my father; my little sister was by another man, the one my mother ended up marrying; and my little brother was by a different man.

I also noticed while growing up that my mother did not really have any friends. I guess that was due to a lack of trust or something that had happened to her in her life. Whenever I would say something about my friends, she would sarcastically say, "You don't have no friends. I am your friend." So we see that my mother had covenant-breaking spirits, spirits of fornication, adultery, rejection and abuse attached to her bloodline. The reason I associate the spirit of rejection with my mother is because my father was having babies with her and another woman at the same time. I am sure both of them had to be experiencing some form of rejection. Also, when my mother was growing up, she and her sister lived with their father and his mother. My mother's father was a police officer and he was half Jewish and half black.

My mother said that she and her sister typically raised themselves due to their father working a lot of different shifts. His mother was sick so she couldn't take care of them. My mother and her sister had to spend their young years taking care of her. My mother's mother and father got divorced when my mother was seven years old. However, I was told that both parents were still in their lives. I also vaguely remember either my grandmother or my aunt Della telling me that my grandmother would walk a very long distance to see her daughters' every day. The walk was so far and long it would make you cry.

My grandfather also married another lady and I can remember going over to their house many times when we were little. I also have an uncle who was my grandfather's son by another woman, who we will be discussing later on in this book. Again, I am not telling these things to bring any shame or embarrassment to anybody; I am only trying to paint a picture of all the spirits that I have had to fight in my life that will continue to operate in the generations to come if my other family members and I refuse to walk in the authority that has been given to us by God. I am also trying to show others how to identify and gather information concerning the spirits that might try to operate in their lives and upcoming generations, due to the sins of their forefathers. Demons don't care how old we are in age. They will still try to operate in our lives. It appears that my mother's father had some playboy spirits in him as well.

Many times, we as people judge and criticize one another because of things that we struggle with in life, when none of us had the ability to vote on what generational spirits we were going to have to fight or who our parents, grandparents, or great-grandparents and so on were going to be. If we could have voted, I am sure we all would have preferred to come from a lineage of saints.

All spirits that are passed through our bloodlines are not bad spirits. My mother never had an alcohol problem or a problem with drugs and she always tried to keep us dressed real nice. I can still vaguely remember two of the wash dresses she would wear around the house and the beautiful

Easter outfits we would get year after year due to the sacrifices my mother made to make sure her girls looked nice. Although my father had a lot of bad spirits on his bloodline, he was a businessman. Being a businessman can be a good thing. It just depends on what type of business you are running. He owned taverns and we know that is not the will of the Lord.

I do not really know all the type of sicknesses that ran through my father's bloodline, but I do know that my grandmother on my mother's side and her three sisters had battled breast cancer. This is the reason I said we must continually pray and bind generational spirits and sicknesses, because even though I was saved and serving the Lord, that spirit of breast cancer literally snuck up on me in 2009. It is now 2015 and the Lord has kept me here. I could not believe that I, being filled with the Holy Ghost, had ended up battling breast cancer. However, the Word of the Lord tells us that whatever we bind on earth will be bound in heaven and whatever we loose on earth will be loosed in heaven.

My Childhood
Rebellion is the major reason I believe that I ended up going through a lot of the things I went through. I was a very rebellious child. I rebelled against the Lord, my mother, grandmother, the law and all who were in authority. I was determined to do my own thing and refused to let anybody tell me what to do. Everything that we do that God does not like is an act of rebellion.

Fighting
I can remember all the way back to when I was four years old. I had a little friend who lived right next door to us in a four-unit apartment building and we lived in a four-family flat. My little girlfriend would hit me and hurry up and run

to her building with her short little legs and lock the door because she knew if I caught her I was going to beat her up. It was amazing how she outran me, considering the fact that I was taller than her. Once she would make it safely behind the locked door, I would get so mad because I couldn't catch her. I would pound on the glass door while she would be spitting and licking her tongue on the glass. This was the first manifestation of anger, fighting and violence that I can remember manifesting in my life, although I was too young to decipher what was really going on. At that time, I did not realize that the same fighting demons that were on the inside of my father were now manifesting through me. When I got much older, in my twenties, I pushed a glass door so hard while I was angry that I accidentally almost killed myself. Not realizing my own strength, as I was trying to push the door open, my whole arm went through the glass, and I cut an artery, tendons, nerves and ligaments. People who have spirits of anger and violence are very strong, because it is a demonic spirit.

Stealing
The second thing that I can remember doing wrong was stealing some of my big sister's Christmas money because she had gotten more money than I had gotten. I do not think I was any more than six or seven years old at the time. As time progressed I later became a professional shoplifter and then a professional pickpocket. Stealing was another one of the sins of my father that had visited me. Remember, he used to steal while he was working for the railroad. My father was definitely city slick and a hustler. Although I didn't really know him, I inherited the same reputation when I was growing up.

I was very rebellious and determined to do whatever I wanted to do in my life. My rebellion, bad choices and lifestyle caused my mother and grandmother a lot of heartaches and pain. My grandmother was sanctified and filled with the Holy Ghost, but my mother was not saved at all during the younger years of my life. I was raised in the same house with both of them. We lived in an apartment at 5552 Palm Street in St. Louis, Missouri. Although my grandmother was saved, I don't think she had as much knowledge about spiritual things as we do today. But she would always say to me that I looked just like my father, acted like him and lied like him.

I was so bad and rebellious that when it would be raining, thundering and lightening, I would jump in the bed with my grandmother because I knew she was saved. She would tell me there was no reason for me to jump in the bed with her because she couldn't help me if the Lord was going to do anything to me. The last time I can remember jumping in the bed with my grandmother while it was storming was when I was about thirteen years old and in about the eighth grade. That was far too old for me to still be jumping in bed with my grandmother. All bad children tend to appear to be very scared of the dark and thunder and lightning.

The apartment that we lived in was only a one-bedroom apartment. At first it was just my grandmother, my mother, my big sister and me. We were very poor. My mother slept on a let-out couch in the living room while my big sister and I slept in a full-size bed with our grandmother in the bedroom. Then my mother met my stepfather, who had a car, and they got married. He moved in with us and slept on the let-out couch with my mother. My mother got pregnant with my little sister, who is five years younger than me. The marriage didn't last long. I think he lived with us for a little over a year. We lived the majority of our lives with all women in our house. We never had a male or father figure living with us, except that short time my little sister's dad was there.

I don't remember what I had done, but I can remember my little sister's father smacking me real hard one night while I was sitting in the kitchen. I think he was listening to the ball game on the radio, and I must have been making a lot of noise. One thing I will admit though, and that is I was very rebellious; but as far as I was concerned, he wasn't my daddy, so he didn't have any right to put his hands on me. Well anyway, before I knew it he was moving out. I don't know what happened between the two of them, but I do know that whatever happened between my mother, my stepfather and my father who was before him left my mother in a place that she no longer wanted to be bothered with another relationship period.

Of course, because I didn't know any better, I would encourage her to get in a relationship. My mother was a very beautiful, attractive, high yellow woman with big beautiful eyes. One day while we were standing at the bus stop, a man pulled over in a gray and black Cadillac. He dropped us off where we were going, and that is when their relationship began. He ended up being my little brother's father eventually. When he started coming over, it appeared that the rebellion in my life began to increase even more, along with rejection, because now it appeared to me that my mother was spending more time with him than with us. Well, I was about twelve years old at the time and I would really give that man a hard time. Due to the spirit of rejection that was already operating in my life, I was trying my best to run him away.

Also, while I was twelve years old, in the sixth grade, one of my friends had moved back to St. Louis, Missouri, from

Los Angeles, California. At lunchtime she would take me over to her house and teach me how to smoke cigarettes. My friend had gotten so fast while she was living in Los Angeles that she could smoke cigarettes so good at the age of twelve that she knew how to form "O's" while she was blowing the cigarette smoke out of her mouth. I am sure the devil used that attraction of seeing her blow "O's" out of her mouth as a tool to entice me to want to learn how to smoke. One day when I was late coming back to our sixth-grade classroom, after taking my daily smoking lessons, I took it upon myself to write my teacher a note stating that it was from my mother that read:

"Please forgive Jacqueline for being late for class. Next time she is late I am going to give her a whooping."

I had no idea that I had spelled whipping wrong. The teacher read the note out loud in front of the whole class and they all fell out laughing at me. This also resulted from me thinking I was halfway slick!

On another occasion, while I was at home, the thought came to my mind to go in the bathroom and smoke a cigarette, so I did. When I left the bathroom, all the cigarette smoke made an exit with me. My mother not only smelled the cigarette smoke, she saw it. I wonder why the devil that told me to go in the bathroom to smoke the cigarette didn't at least tell me to raise up the bathroom window so that the smoke would blow out so that I would not have gotten busted. Now I realize that the enemy (devil) always makes suggestions for us to do something stupid, but he never tells us the consequences we are going to suffer, due to our wrong choices. Although the devil's suggestions may sound good, we have got to realize that he hates us all and that he is not our friend. He makes those suggestions so that we can get in trouble and mess up our lives. He loves to see us strung out on drugs, depressed, living in poverty, or spending the majority of our lives in jail.

While I was still in the sixth grade, one of my friends and I that walked to school together every day decided that we were going to play hooky from school that particular day. So we stole a pack of her mother's cigarettes because her mother and father bought cartons of cigarettes. She would steal a pack and then stack them back in the carton so that her mother would not notice that a pack was missing. The reason we stole her mother's cigarettes was because her mother smoked KOOL cigarettes and her father smoked PALL MALL.

Anyway, as we were sitting there smoking our cigarettes and listening to some of our favorite songs by Michael Jackson, someone knocked on the door. We peeped out and it was my grandmother. I did not know how she knew I had played hooky from school, but I lied and told her that I had gotten sick when I got to my friend's house to pick her up for school. She believed me and took me home and fixed me some breakfast. So as you can see, even at that age I had already began to become a big manipulator and habitual liar as well. Demons run in packs. My grandmother would always say if you lie you will also steal.

Also at age twelve I would also stand on the corner with the neighborhood wine heads and drink Rosie O'Grady and MD 20/20, better known as Mad Dog, which was probably the cheapest wine you could buy from the store in those days. I came in the house so drunk one night I can remember washing my hair and sitting up under one of those old portable hair dryers with the rubber nodule that connected the dryer to the heating cap that blew the hot air from the dryer to the plastic heating cap. As I sat under the dryer drunk, I fell asleep with my arm resting on the hot rubber hose that the hot heat was blowing through. When I finally woke up, I had a big nasty blister on my arm. There is still a mark on my arm from that blister until this day. I have a lot of battle scars, but this was my first one. When we are living in sin, bad things happen to us. If I had not been drunk at twelve years old and had been in bed getting ready for school the next day, like the average twelve-year-old child would have been doing, my arm never would have gotten burnt.

It was extremely rough growing up in St. Louis, especially if you didn't have any big brothers. My big sister and I were only one year apart and our baby sister was just a newborn baby. My little brother was not even born yet. I started fighting a lot because you had to fight in the neighborhood I grew up in, or else you were guaranteed to get bullied every day. Since we didn't have a big brother, I decided I was going to be the big brother in my family because I was not accepting any whippings, especially from children who were the same age as I was. My first fight at school was with a boy, because at that age (twelve years old), when a boy liked you and you didn't like him back, he would express his anger by constantly picking on you. That often consisted of following you home every day and pulling your hair.

One day a boy was picking on me. When I decided to defend myself, for some reason I was able to win that fight. I knew that if I hadn't won that fight, it was going to be real hard for me in school. I didn't have any trouble out of that boy anymore. I was also a tomboy when I was growing up. I liked shooting marbles, which was a boy's game. I didn't realize at the time that it was a spirit in me that enjoyed beating boys at whatever they did. After getting saved, I learned that it was just a spirit of Jezebel that I believe most black women ended up having to fight to get set free from, especially if their mother was the head of the household, a single parent. A Jezebel spirit is a spirit that likes to run things and always be in control.

At the elementary school I attended, there was a big girl who went to our school who was a bully. I am not going to lie; I was terrified of her. Not only that, she had a terrible body odor. For those two reasons alone, I did not want to get tangled up in a fight with her. The back of her neck was real black and she slicked her hair down in the back with MURRAY'S hair grease because we didn't have hair gel back then. Well, one day she sent me a note telling me how she was going to beat me up after school, and I was sitting there at my desk scared. However, I looked at her and tore the note up in front of her face, as if to say, "I will be waiting for you outside."

Thank God when we got out of school, she was nowhere in sight and she never sent me another note. She had to weigh about 250 pounds, while I could not have weighed any more than 110 pounds at the max. Children can be so cruel at times. If you dressed better than the other children, they had it in for you. If you had more lunch money than the other children, they had it in for you. If you looked better than the other children, they had it in for you. Growing up was really a challenge back then, so I can imagine what our youth are going through now.

After that episode, one day I had to fight my girlfriend who had taught me how to smoke cigarettes. My big sister was nowhere to be found, but my opponent's big sister was there. Although my big sister was not there, my big sister's girlfriend was there who had a lot of brothers. Their family had a very bad reputation and nobody messed with their family. My sister's girlfriend looked at my opponent's big sister and everybody in the crowd and made an announcement. Her exact words were, "My opponent and I are going to have to fight until one of us gives up," and that is exactly what happened. Sadly to say, it looked like no matter how bad I beat that girl, she would not give up. We fought so long that I was tired, breathing hard and all out of breath. Her sister was crying and begging her to please give up. She knew that she was no match for my big sister's friend and that she was too afraid to fight her, so all she could do was cry and beg her sister to please give up.

My opponent was stubborn as a mule. I was beating her so bad that I began to feel sorry for her myself. When she wouldn't give up, I started banging her head against the curb. Her stubborn butt still wouldn't give up as her poor big sister continued crying out, "Please give up . . ., please give up . . ." I then had to result to hitting her in her face with a brick that was lying on the curb. That was when she finally gave up. She was a pretty yellow girl and I really didn't want things to go as far as they did. I have never really wanted to hurt anyone, but I was certainly not going to allow anybody to hurt me either. After the fight was finally over, my big sister's friend walked me home and she was so proud of me for winning that fight. When we made it to our apartment, because my face had a few scratches on it, my mother said being sarcastic, "It sure looks like somebody got a hold of your behind today." My sister's friend told her, "No, Ms. Henderson, you should see the girl your daughter was fighting. Your daughter beat the mess out of that girl and she is in way worse shape than your daughter is in." Then she went on bragging and being very descriptive about everything that happened in the fight. Well, I didn't know that this was just the beginning of my fighting career. I became a good fighter in the world. I had enough of them to be an expert. I have always been a nice sweet person and I have never initiated a fight. However, if someone did something to me, I believe the spirits of anger, rage and violence that I had inherited from my father would take over. I would literally lose control and have black outs, especially if someone stole something from me. I have always been a free-hearted person and all they had to do was ask. I will give a person the shirt off of my back, but please don't try to take it!

I thought after I got saved my fighting days would finally be over—not true. It took me so long to get delivered from fighting after I got saved that I am ashamed to tell you how long it took. I literally cried and begged God to help me, because I felt so stupid when I had my last episode as old as I was spiritually.

The devil constantly fights us in order to try to get us to act out of character once we are saved, and we must learn how to fight him back. We can't fight him physically; we must fight him spiritually. The fighting spirits that were probably passed down from my father eventually worked out for my good. God has now given me the strength to not put my physical hands on anybody. God loves fighters. He just doesn't like for us to fight in the flesh or fight each other. The Lord actually delights in saving fighters and training them how to fight in the Spirit so that He can raise them up to become spiritual warriors. Our God is a man of war. The devil is making a fool out of so many people by having us killing and fighting each other, instead of the demons inside the people. In the end, when the devil is finished, both parties are defeated. One ends up dead or badly hurt, and the other one probably ends up making a career out of the penitentiary. And in all actuality, if they don't repent they end up going to hell.

This foolishness not only affects the one who is killed or hurt badly, and the one who went to the penitentiary, it also affects their family members and friends. So who really won? The devil won, and he is laughing every time he has the opportunity to make a fool out of somebody. He is laughing every time he has the opportunity to influence us to hurt each other and mess up our lives and the lives of others. It is time for us to stop allowing the devil to trick us. It is time for us to quit allowing the devil to make a fool out of us. The devil does people just as he did me. He makes them try to make a reputation for themselves in front of all of their peers, and they really end up hurting somebody by trying to be tough. Then when they end up in jail or the penitentiary, all of their so-called friends that they were showing off for are nowhere to be found and forget all about them. They do not receive one letter or visit from them, or one penny on their books for commissary. I am a firm believer that a lot of this gang violence will stop once we turn our anger in the right direction, toward the devil instead of each other. Anger will make us do and say things that we will be sorry for, for the rest of our lives.

It is time for us to deal with the spirit of anger in our lives that causes us to do and say things that we will regret later. Just think for a minute and ask God where that anger came from. Why are you angry? What happened in your life that has caused you to be so angry? You may be angry because you feel like you have been dealt a bad hand in life. Well, I want you to know that if you turn your life over to the Lord, He will deal you a new hand. God had to show me one day how stupid it looks for a spiritual person to be arguing with a demonic spirit on the inside of somebody. I don't have to have the last word today. I now have the power to look at the other party and not have to prove to them that I am not afraid of them. The devil already knows I am not scared, and he has used that tool far too long to try to get me to act out of character.

Also during this time in my life, instead of going to my grade school, where I should have been going, I would go to high school with my older friends. I also loved hanging out in the dangerous projects where a lot of killing was going on. What a blessing and a miracle it is for me to be alive today! The projects in St. Louis were not a place for anyone to live, so you know it certainly wasn't a place for a twelve-year-old girl to be hanging out at. Shapen in iniquity and destined for failure, sin began to accelerate in my life. Now here I am twelve years old telling, not asking, my mother that I am going to go and spend the night over one of my girlfriend's house every weekend. And that is what I did! I had a strong determination and a strong will. Just like many of you who are reading this book. That is why when we begin to accept and pursue God's will for our lives, the forces of hell cannot stop us from fulfilling the destiny that God has ordained for our lives We all have power that is on the inside of us to do everything that God has called us to do. I would like to believe that it is hidden from us while we are living in darkness because the Bible tells us:

2 Corinthians 4:7

But we have this treasure in earthen vessels, that the excellency of the power may be of God, and not of us.

1 Corinthians 2:9
But as it is written, Eye hath not seen, nor ear heard, neither have entered into the heart of man, the things which God hath prepared for them that love him.

Treasure is usually hidden and if you could just get a glimpse of the treasure that is on the inside of you and the plan that God has for your life, you would tell the devil you have changed your mind about serving him. This is the season that God is causing a holy anger and a payback anointing to come upon the people of God. We are going to pay the devil back for all of the times that he has had the opportunity to make a fool out of us and use us in the past. We are also going to take back everything that he has stolen from us in the name of Jesus.

If you have had a challenge with drugs in your life in the past, maybe the devil stole your integrity. Well, you can take it back right now in the name of Jesus, by force.

Matthew 11:12
And from the days of John the Baptist until now the kingdom of heaven suffereth violence, and the violent take it by force.

Now, there I was, still twelve years old, with a great determination to go and spend the night over my friend's house, where there was no supervision. And in the midst of our madness, God really watched over all of us because anything could have happened to us. Her mother was an alcoholic and she was never home, while we would be in the house with lots of so-called friends, both male and female. We could have gotten gang raped or killed. None of us girls were having sex yet, and the only reason we were not having sex yet was because we took pride in saying that we were virgins.

When I was thirteen years old, we moved to our new low-income apartment and I had to transfer to another grade school. And now that my big sister had her own room, my rejection was really beginning to show, although I was really rejected from the womb, because my daddy tried to get my mother to take some toothache medicine in order to abort me.

After I graduated from eighth grade, age fourteen, I was determined to go to Soldan High School, one of the most notorious high schools in the city of St. Louis. Soldan was not the high school I was supposed to go to due to the district we lived in. But of course with a determination like mine, I was going to make it happen. I was determined to go to the high school that my friends were going to that I had rebelliously been hanging out with. Now here I am gang banging, smoking reefer, drinking alcohol, popping pills, taking acid and stealing grandmother's valiums to get high, living a fast life destined for failure because of course I did not know that things would only get worse and worse due to my own rebellion. As a freshman in high school, when most girls really start having a crush on the opposite sex, I was finally invited over to his house, the guy that I had a crush on. I had no idea he was going to force me into his bedroom in the big mansion they lived in and make me have sex with him.

I was intrigued that their family lived in a mansion, not

knowing that the family had only adopted the young man who had literally raped me. Whoever would have imagined that something like that would happen at a house where people were so well to do? My family had never lived in anything but an apartment all of our lives. I can still remember as if it was only yesterday—my stepfather rolling soda bottles across the floor trying to kill the mice that had invaded our one bedroom apartment we lived in before we moved into our fresh, newly built, three-bedroom, low-income apartment for people who could not afford to pay market rent. That was really a come-up for us considering our prior situation. My mother had her own bedroom, my older sister had her own bedroom and my grandmother, my little sister and I shared the other bedroom. In the bedroom that my grandmother, my little sister and I shared, we all had our own separate beds finally. However, I thought that since my big sister and I were only a little over one year apart, we would have shared a bedroom. Sometimes you would be surprised at the little things that children pay attention too no matter what age they are. Parents pay close attention to the things you do in order to make sure you are not doing things that appear like you are showing more favoritism toward one of your children than the others. This can cause them to begin to look for love in all the wrong places. We all have a blind side. Pray and ask the Lord to show you yourself.

Also, while I was in rebellion spending the night over my girlfriend's house, whose mother was an alcoholic, I met another girlfriend who ended up being my best friend while both of us were in rebellion spending the night over our friend's house. She and I would leave the high school we were supposed to be attending, so that we could hang out at Northwest High School on the north side. Well, I eventually got kicked out of Soldan High School for cutting classes and getting caught in too many hall sweeps. A hall sweep is when all the security guards, teachers and the principal would sweep the halls to catch all the bad students who were supposed to be in class. Since I was put out of Soldan, I ended up going to Sumner High School, the high school where I was supposed to be going to in the first place. I didn't last there but a little over a year. I forgot what happened, but I ended up going to Lincoln Opportunity, which was a high school for bad children.

I later ended up dropping out of high school and went to work as a waitress at Walgreens. My excuse was my mother didn't buy me any clothes, so I wanted to work and buy my own clothes. The truth of the matter was, when my mother did finally try to buy me some clothes one day, I called myself being nickel dime slick and took them back to Sears. They gave me a refund slip to be able to spend later. I tried changing the amount on the refund slip so that I would have more money to spend, which caused my mother to end up losing all her money because the store took the refund slip back and would not honor it at all. Of course we were too poor to suffer any losses like that, but I guess that was the price I had to pay for trying to be slick. I ended up with nothing.

Although I went to work as a waitress, after a while I couldn't even tell you what happened with that. I was the type of person who simply lost interest in things after a while. I had never finished anything. I later ended up getting a job at a factory that paid good money at the time. My best friend would walk from her sister's house where she had ended up living to bring me lunch for work. I also had a young man who lived about five blocks away, from the low-income apartment that we lived in at the time, taking me to work every day. He was a very well-mannered young man who seemed to come from a wholesome family, but of course he wasn't my type. I was using him for a ride to get back and forth to work every day. And when I would get out of his car, I would say thank you. To this day he has never even gotten more than a handshake. I had several young men like that; I guess you could say that I thought they were my personal chauffeurs. Of course I was not stupid. I knew they wanted to be more than just a friend to me, but let's face it, they were not my type. I can remember one whose teeth looked green, and he had the nerve to ask me for a kiss one day. I have to admit it myself. I was a bad child and I ended up paying for everything I did either then, or later in life. For some reason I was only attracted to hard-core gangster type guys and big-time drug dealers that had a whole lot of money.

In addition, I had a problem with jumping in and out of cars with strangers to get a ride or just smoke their marijuana up. One night I was bored, and I was walking around in the neighborhood and I met this guy. He had some reefer, so I got in his car and was kicking it with him because those were the little silly games I played with men. I knew that I had no intentions on having sex with any of them. This guy drove me all the way to his apartment in Brentwood, Missouri, and insisted that I come in his apartment. I told him I would wait in the car, but since he kept on insisting, I went on in. I can't remember what reason he gave me that I needed to come on in. Well, once I got inside he began to try to seduce me. When I went for the door, he grabbed me by the back of my hair and literally pulled me down to the floor backwards. I was still pretty much a virgin because I had only really had sex twice, once when I tried it on my own, and then with the guy I called myself liking who lived in the mansion forced me too. Sex was too painful to me for me to continue trying willfully in the beginning.

Well, this man in Brentwood, Missouri abused me everywhere and every way he wanted too in his apartment. I was so sure that when he finished with me he was going to kill me, so something told me to pretend that I liked him and everything that he was doing to me. I told him as he was driving me back home that I wanted to see him again the next day; of course, I was just lying. When he dropped me off at our apartment, I was too afraid to tell my mother what happened, and I didn't want to call the police because I had remembered watching a movie on television that Elizabeth Montgomery played in, where this man had raped her, and when he got through with her on the witness stand, he made the jury believe that she had been pursuing him, and he won the case. I was sure that same thing would have happened to me. Let's face it, I was not saved back then, and although I was not regularly having sex, my attire was saying something altogether different. Not only that, I got in the man's car on my own just to get a free high. He didn't force me into his car. I guess I could say that maybe I got what I deserved from playing so many games with men that I had played games with in the past that I knew I was not interested in.

The next day when I got out of bed, I could hardly walk because the man had abused my little young body so bad the day before. I was too embarrassed to tell anybody, so when my girlfriends came over so that we could walk up to the gym to play a game called horse we used to play I went anyway. HORSE was a game that consisted of shooting a basketball in a hoop until you spell HORSE. I was in so much pain as I straggled along as we walked toward the gym. I was trying to walk normal so that no one would figure out that something was wrong. It would seem like we would learn from lessons like these, but I guess because we have gotten away with the games that we have played so many times before we ran into the wrong guy, it created in us the courage to continue to try it again and again. Or maybe, after a certain amount of time has passed from the bad experiences that we had, we somehow end up either forgetting the last incident or getting what I would like to call selective amnesia.

Well, one night, this rich white guy picked me up in a very expensive sports car. We were very poor, so I probably thought that maybe this rich guy was my way out of living in poverty and could make my life a whole lot better than it was. He took me to his house and we were really getting along real good at first. I have always had the type of personality that if a person met me one time, they would feel so comfortable talking to me that it would seem as if we had been knowing each other for years. Then the guy began to tell me about what a fit his parents would have if they knew he was socializing with a black girl. As he continued talking, his conversation began to get spookier and spookier.

I began to get scared because I didn't know if he was going to kill me or hurt me in some kind of way. He appeared to be becoming very satanic. Well saved by the bell, his telephone happened to ring. It was one of his family members telling him that his sister had been in a very bad car accident and he needed to make it to the hospital as quickly as he could. As he was probably contemplating taking my life, the way things sounded from the phone call he had just received, his sister was fighting for her life. He drove me back to the city and dropped me off, but if the truth were told, I believe that the good Lord had spared my life again that night. In my younger years I was very attractive. I had long beautiful black hair and a cute shape that would literally end up costing me my life if it was not for the Lord having a better plan for me.

My mother and I didn't get along, so I ended up staying with some other close friends of mine who were twins (both girls) and their mother was a church lady. The twins came from a very large family. There were three boys and six girls in their family altogether and the twins were the babies of the family. Of course one of the twins and I were closer than the other one and I. The twins were also bigger than many of the other children at the high school we attended and people knew not to mess with them. There was one young lady at our high school who was very dark skinned and actually had muscles like a man that wanted to fight me for no reason at all. My friend, one of the twins, let everybody know it was going to be a fair fight and she looked at me and told me I had better win that fight or else I was going to have to fight her and I actually won the fight. However, the girl I was fighting was bigger and looked as though she was much stronger than me.

One of the twins and I used to stay up all night playing Blackjack, Black Deuce and Tunk for money until one of us would win all of the money. Another spirit inherited from my father. However, my friends and I stayed high on beer, weed, and as time progressed, Sherman Sticks. Although the twins didn't indulge, I was taking acid, valiums, and had begun to start snorting cocaine, which eventually led me to smoking cocaine later in life. One of our other friends who lived across the street from the twins had a stepbrother who always stayed in jail that liked me. I knew he had money because he was always flirting with me and trying to get me to accept money from him but I wouldn't.

I had never played any type of games with this guy, because first of all, he was one of my friends stepbrother; secondly, he lived right across the street from my friends, the twins, that I was living with; and thirdly, I didn't trust him because he seemed to be far too obsessed over me. I knew if he liked me as much as he did, without me giving him the time of day, if I would have strung him along and then tried to break the relationship off, he probably would have been the type to try to abuse or possibly kill me. One day he called my friend's house and asked to speak to me. He began to threaten me and tell me that if I did not come over to his house that night and take care of my business as I had promised him I would, he was going to hurt me. I got scared because I had already thought he was borderline crazy.

As I began to tell my girlfriend, one of the twins, who I was living with at the time, she laughed so hard that she could hardly stand up. She then told me that the guy had called over to their house the day before, and she had pretended like she was me and had told him to slide some money up under the door for me and he had done it. Now you know that guy had to be awfully obsessed to fall for something like that. I had to explain to him that it was not me who took his money, but he didn't believe me and was very angry because of it. My own friend could have gotten me hurt behind that situation. We were all smoking so much marijuana and Sherman sticks during that time of our lives that I believe we were all a little touched in the mind, doing dumb things without thinking about what the consequences could have been.

Also, at age sixteen, I began to notice that everywhere I began to go, it was somebody from a church trying to witness to me. And believe me, I did not want to hear it, and I did not have time. I had already spent the majority of my life living in the house with a sanctified grandmother who would start speaking in tongues, while laying her hands on my head. I had no idea what she was saying when she was speaking in those tongues. And when those old church ladies would come and try to tell me God had a calling on my life, I thought I was too young and too cute to be saved. I felt like they had already had their fun, and now they were trying to keep me from having mine; and now since they were old, they wanted me to go to church like an old lady like them. I had no idea that God speaks through people. Now I love the true prophets of the Lord. They are a blessing to the saved and the unsaved. However, I still had no idea God was calling me. So God just let me continue to live my life thinking I was too cute to be saved, and hanging out with people older than me. God just allowed the devil to keep whipping me because He knew the things that I was going to encounter in life, due to leaning to my own understanding, would eventually run me to Him.

Still at age sixteen, one day, I went over to another one of my girlfriend's house. One of her big brothers called himself liking me, and I not only thought he was so fine, he was. My girlfriend would be so mad at her brother that she would beg him to leave me, her friend, alone because she grew up with him and knew him much better than I did. As a matter of fact, she knew that during that time of our lives, all of her older brothers were not any good. They were dope fiends and natural-born hustlers. They came from a real big family and there were about twelve or thirteen of them. I knew we were poor, but they were even poorer than we were.

One day the brother who called himself liking me took me with him and a dope fiend lady who was a professional booster (shoplifter) to a store. After she had stolen the majority of the merchandise she wanted to steal for herself, she took me to another store, stole a girdle, and told me to put it on. She then taught me how to stuff clothes down in the girdle and walk out of the stores with everything I thought I wanted. It was in the summer of 1976 when those umbrella dresses were out. Those dresses were so wide; if you knew how to walk properly, no one would ever be able to detect that you had anything stuffed up under it. After we left the stores that day, she sold all her merchandise she had stolen. I went to the hotel with her and him and they began to shoot dope. Mind you, I was still only sixteen years old. Neither one of them tried to influence me into shooting dope. I am sure, now that I have had an encounter with being a dope fiend myself, it wasn't because they felt I was too young for them to turn me out. It was because they wanted it all for themselves. I wasn't interested anyway and I thank God I wasn't interested at that age in my life. As I think about things now, I realize if I had become an alcoholic while I was drinking at age twelve, I probably would have ended up with cirrhosis of the liver by age forty. If I had started shooting dope at age sixteen, all of my teeth would be rotten, and I know I would look much older than I look right now.

Now, my reputation had really blown up in the city because I had become one of the coldest boosters (shoplifters) in the city of St. Louis. I had been taught by the best, a dope fiend woman who had to go to any extent to get her fix every day. I not only knew how to stuff clothes in a girdle and walk out of the stores, I would also take clothes off a clothes rack and put them straight into a shopping bag and walk out. Well, here I am now considered a top-flight booster and now I could have everything that Momma couldn't afford to buy me. I was so good at stealing that I had a fence man, who would buy all of my merchandise at one set price, along with other customers that would put their orders in on a daily basis as well. I had jewelry, a pocket full of money, I wore designer silk and satin shirts, designer jeans, designer dresses and designer everything, so of course I had a big reputation in the city.

At that time I was also border-line crazy because my friends and I would smoke Sherman sticks like we were smoking cigarettes. When it was time for us to go boosting, we would say we were getting ready to go to work. We would say that we are getting ready to go in those white folks stores and steal all of their stuff. I had gotten to the point that I had told my poor grandmother, that was already worried about me, that I was never going to work for the white man and that I would always be a hustler.

My grandmother was saved, sanctified and filled with the Holy Ghost. And due to the lack of attention that I was getting in the family, she always made up the slack and tried to make me feel as though I was her favorite. I could steal so good that it was a long time before I had ever gone to jail for boosting, but I can remember the first time I went to jail as if it just happened yesterday. I was so afraid that I had bitten off all of my fingernails and was getting ready to start working on my toes. Then a bondsman came and got me out of jail. The guy that I was going with at that time, not my friend's brother who had the dope fiend lady to teach me how to steal, had paid the bondman.

After meeting the bondman, I later started dating him. He was an older man who was very well to do. As we began to meet each other and talk, I found out that he knew my grandfather, who had been a police officer when he was alive. His comment was that he knew my grandfather would be turning over in his grave if he knew he was having sex with his granddaughter. By my friend being a bondsman, a lot of his customers were prostitutes who worked on the stroll in St. Louis. When he would be taking me home, after having our affair, he would ride down the stroll to see if he saw any of the prostitutes working that still owed him money from previously bonding them out of jail. I would duck my head down in the car because I was so full of pride and I didn't want anybody to see me riding on what we called the stroll. This would upset my friend the bondsman and he would make smart comments like, "Why are you holding your head down." I had no idea at that time that later on in life, I would be one of those women working as a prostitute on a stroll.

I can also remember on another occasion I had gotten me a ride to go boosting and I took another girl with me who had no experience at all at stealing. We had been to so many stores that our driver's car trunk was so full that there was not any room to put anything else in it. Of course, due to greed and showing off my boosting skills, I wanted to go to one more store. As the time for the stores to close was quickly approaching I took some clothes off the rack, put them in a shopping bag, got in the car, and as we drove off the parking lot, the red lights on the police car began to start flashing for us to pull over. When we got to the police station and they saw all the merchandise we had stolen, they were flabbergasted. The young lady who was with me immediately told the police that everything was mine and I was trying to influence her and teach her how to steal.

After our fingerprints came back and we finally got released from jail, I went home. I really can't remember how my poor grandmother found out I had caught a case. However, when I went to court, I lied and told the judge that the reason I had stolen all those clothes was because I was trying to go to Job Corps. I was really a habitual liar when I was not saved, and I was really a good one. Anyway, my poor grandmother committed to paying the fine that they were charging me to stay out of jail from her little social security check she was receiving every month, until the fine was paid off. I still feel bad about that to this day.

When I was growing up, I had an uncle, my mother's half-brother, who was always getting into a lot of trouble doing burglaries and robberies with his friends. His father, who was my grandfather, my mother's father, was a police officer and he would always get my uncle out of jail no matter what he did. I briefly heard my mother telling their father one day that he needed to let my uncle go to jail and do some jail time so that maybe he would quit doing the things that he was doing, since he knew my grandfather was going to keep getting him out. One day my uncle and his friends had done a burglary and the police didn't catch him. If I remember correctly, he was supposed to have been hiding real good. I believe he was hiding behind the air conditioner in the store. However, when the police were getting ready to leave he gave himself up. So after that stunt, he did have to go to the Jefferson City Penitentiary in Jefferson City, Missouri, to serve some time.

I was still sixteen years old when my favorite uncle got out of jail and ended up being one of the biggest dope dealers in the city. Of course, I wanted to hang out with my favorite uncle everywhere he went. I carried the key to the glove compartment in the car where he kept his pistol so that if the police pulled us over, he could tell them he didn't have the key to the glove compartment because his car was registered in his wife's mother's name. We would be going to his dope spots to drop his drugs off and pick his money up, horseback riding and to the rifle range, where he demanded that I learn how to shoot all types of artillery, including rifles with scopes on them that kicked so hard that one of his friends almost put his eye out while trying to shoot one of them. When I would tell my uncle I did not want to shoot the rifles, that I only wanted to shoot the pistols, his reply was, "What are you going to do when some real trouble kicks off?" So I was obedient to my uncle and would practice shooting all the other artillery along with the rifles with the scopes on them with my uncle and his workers.

Although my uncle sold heroin, he always told me not to ever mess with heroine. I can even remember one day he let all of my friends snort some and they started throwing up, but he would not let me snort any. I was so mad at him that day I felt like he was doing me wrong. But now that I have had the experience of being a heroin addict, I guess my uncle did love me for not allowing me to snort any of it, because he knew how addictive it was. However, although he encouraged me not to ever touch any heroin, due to the notorious lifestyle he was living, he did not live long enough to protect me from what would end up being my worst nightmare later on in life, HEROIN.

I loved my uncle so much. I thought he was one of the slickest, smoothest and handsomest men in the world. I can remember us going to this run-down hotel one day where he got one of his workers to get in the car while I and one of his other workers were already in the car. My uncle held a pistol to the guy's head and began questioning him about some things. The poor guy was literally crying and begging for his life. I just knew my uncle was going to kill him that night, but he ended up taking him back to the run-down hotel where he lived. I guess they made some type of arrangements to resolve whatever had my uncle so upset.

One day my uncle and I had went to one of his dope houses and he had gone out to his car to get something. I believe it was some of his drugs that he was going to leave for the lady whose house we were at to sell or either put up for him.

Anyway, somebody must have told the police that my uncle was a drug dealer and where he was. People always snitched on each other back then due to jealousy, or if they were trying to get a sentence reduced. Well, my uncle said the police started running toward him and grabbed him. He said to the police, "Not me, man, it was him," and the police kept running looking for somebody not knowing that they had the right man.

One night my girlfriends and I went to a house party. I got into an altercation with one of the girls in their house and their whole family jumped on me. My friends that were with me were able to get me in the car that we came in. We knew if those people would have killed us in their house, they would not have gotten charged for the crime. I went to my uncle's house and asked him to give me a pistol, but he wouldn't give me one. The next day my friends and I went to Forest Park on Hippy Hill, where everybody hung out in the summertime. I was informed by one of my friends that they had seen the girl I was fighting the night before. Back then I somehow always kept me a pair of brass knuckles, and I also had a chain that particular day. I climbed up the hill and found the girl that I was mainly fighting when her and her family jumped on me. I started beating her with the chain and she began to run for her life. She knew we was not inside her house that day.

Although my uncle didn't give me the gun the night I asked him for it, I loved him so much that I can remember the day he got murdered as if it just happened yesterday. It was real early in the morning when we got the call saying he was dead. I was told that wherever he was, he had called his wife and told her he was so tired that he needed to lie down on the couch where he was to take a nap before he drove home. A young man supposedly shot him while he was asleep.

Everybody was talking about how much of a coward the guy was that shot him, because he shot him while he was asleep. It was all on the news and in the newspaper. After I found out that his body had finally been transported to the funeral home and was ready for viewing, I immediately went to view his body. I sat up at the funeral home talking to him and asking him questions like, "What am I supposed to do now?" as he lay there in his casket. Yes, I was talking to the dead, but I didn't know any better. I was crying so bad that when my mother finally got me to go home, I slept so hard that I believed they had given me a sedative or something to make me sleep so that I would not be able to go to the funeral and burial the next day. I believe this was done not only because of how hard I took my uncle's death, but also because they were afraid there would be some foul play, due to the lifestyle my uncle lived. When I woke up, I was extremely upset. I really told them off because they had deprived me of the last time I would ever be able to see my favorite uncle again. However, I just found out recently that they didn't even have a funeral for the safety of the family.

I was really a bad child and I took my poor mother through the ringer. My uncle was dead now, I dropped out of high school at sixteen years old and the young man I was going with had a car and he was crazy about me. His mother and father were killed when he was young, so his auntie raised him. One night at the skating ring, one of my friends introduced me to another young man who was liking me, so I quit the other guy who weeks later murdered somebody that worked at his family's store that he felt they had purchased with the money they had gotten due to the death of his parents. He has spent the majority of his life in prison and is still in prison, to this day. He got out for the first crime, and later ended up committing another crime. However, the day I quit him he got so mad at me that he tried to smack me, but I weaved and he missed.

The new guy I started going with had a nice car, and his mother owned a laundromat, liquor store, grocery store, and an ice cream parlor all on the same corner. His mother did not like me because she thought her son was too good for me, and because she knew her son's nose was wide open when it came to me. He was crazy about me and I was crazy about him, so we ended up living together because he and his two sisters stayed in a house by themselves and their mother stayed somewhere else with her husband, who was not the father of any of her children. One of his sisters even told me that he, her brother, could not read or write, in order to try to break us up. The fact that he couldn't read or write didn't matter to me because I loved him; at least I thought I did. During that time, when I was living with my boyfriend and his sisters, I really felt rejected by my mother because she never asked me to move back home. Instead, she would bag me up bags of groceries to take home with me as if she was trying to make sure I was comfortable enough to never come back home again. At least that is the way I deciphered the situation. That was so painful to me.

The young man that I was living with spoiled me at that time and gave me everything I thought I wanted within his power. When we first started going together, he was working at his mother's grocery store, but I don't know what happened with that. Before I knew it we were driving from St. Louis to Chicago to buy some drugs that cost three dollars a pill. He would then sell them for thirteen dollars a pill, so he was really making a lot of money for a minute. However, because his mother did not like me, she did not want to have much to do with her son anymore, so he pretty much had to choose between his mother and me. He chose me, but he eventually ended up losing his drug connects and we ended up going through some pretty rough times together.

Of course at the time, I couldn't see God's hand at work in us, losing the drug connect, but now I do, because if we would have gotten caught with those drugs, I am sure we would have done some hard time in the federal penitentiary. However, when all the money he had made from selling the drugs finally ran out due to us living in elaborate hotels, we had to move in with one of his hard-core drug addict friends who did not have any hot water. It was summertime; thank God it wasn't winter, because I am sure he didn't have any heat either.

We were so broke, we had to boil water on a hot plate to wash up and I had to cook on a hot plate for quite some time. Eventually my boyfriend and his mother started back speaking and she helped my boyfriend and me get an apartment. Eventually he went back to work for her at her store. Then, one of his friends came home from the penitentiary that was very handsome and thought he was a playboy. He came between my boyfriend and me. My boyfriend started hanging out with his friend who was really a bad influence on him. My boyfriend started beating me up because when he would leave me and go hang out with his friend, although my heart was broken, I would put on my little hot pants outfits and go out too in order to make him jealous. He started fighting me so bad and so much I eventually left him. I was about seventeen years old when we started living together and twenty years old when I finally left him. He was really hurt behind me leaving him, so he kept asking his mother to sign for us to get married in order to try to win me back, but she kept refusing.

One day he was trying to prove to me how much he loved

me. He and one of his friends went to stick up an insurance man so that he could try to get the money to buy me a wedding ring. I didn't know anything about what his plans were because I really would have begged him not to go. I heard that he and the insurance man were wrestling over the insurance man's wallet on the ground and his friend shot at the insurance man but the bullet accidentally caught my ex-boyfriend in the neck and he ended up paralyzed on his left side. The doctors said that he would never walk again. As soon as I got the call that he had gotten shot and the seriousness of the injury, I rushed to the hospital because I did not know if he was going to live or die.

Once I arrived at the hospital, he was already out of surgery and was coherent. This girl that was supposed to be working the streets for him was already there when I got there. He immediately told her to leave because he knew if she stayed I was going to leave. He knew my standards were high, and if he thought he had a chance of us getting back together, he knew I didn't believe in sharing my man or any of that other foolishness he had gotten involved in. But because I was young and did not know the difference from being in love with someone and feeling sorry for them, I would go to the hospital faithfully. And when he got out of the hospital, I would go pick him up in his wheelchair. The older women on my job began to talk to me and tell me that I was not with him before he got paralyzed and that I did not owe him anything. They also told me that they knew a lady who was going with a man in a wheelchair and he would grab her and still beat her up bad. Those talks that those older women had with me eventually helped me a lot and I began to come to my senses.

Now due to my ex-boyfriend being paralyzed, all of a sudden his mother had a change of heart and thought it was a good idea for us to get married. That didn't happen though, thanks to the advice from the older women on my job. I was still going to work and going out partying a lot. One summer dark night I was walking home from work and this tall man with finger waves in his hair started walking with me and talking. I was kind of scared to shun him away because I felt like he was up to something. I was not walking in an area that I wanted to take a chance on him snatching me, so I allowed him to follow me home where I was living. I always had a gift of discernment. Even when I was not saved, I could often tell if a person was not up to any good. I was living with my ex-boyfriend's foster sister and her boyfriend. When the man that followed me home came in the house, my paralyzed ex called me on the phone.

After I hung up from talking to him, the man who had followed me home tried to wrap the telephone cord around my neck. He was unsuccessful, so he dragged me out of the house while covering my mouth so that I couldn't scream. I was able to stomp my feet on the table in the house as he was dragging me outside, trying to make a lot of noise so that my ex-boyfriend's foster sister and her boyfriend could hear me. This man was very experienced at what he was doing. He dragged me all the way out of the apartment to the front of the apartment building. I knew this was a life or death situation, so I held on to the gate that surrounded the apartment building with one hand and squeezed his privates as hard as I could with my other hand. He let me go and called me a name while trying to swing on me, so I began to scream as loud as I could. A lot of people that heard me screaming ran outside to see what was going on, and the guy fled on foot.

Because it was something in me that caused me to like hanging out with fast people, on the weekends we would go to a lounge in East St. Louis after the lounges in St. Louis would close where all the hustlers hung out at—pimps, players, drug dealers, prostitutes and boosters. One night when I was at the lounge in East St. Louis, the man who had tried to strangle me was there. When I saw him I got very nervous because I did not know if he had any friends there who were more powerful than the people I knew, or if he was possibly friends with the same people I knew. Well, I had no choice but to find out who he knew as fear continued to grip me, so I went to the top man, the owner of the lounge, who was a pimp that had a lot of women working for him and told him about the incident that had happened when the guy had tried to strangle me. I then pointed the man out to him. The owner and some of his workers called the man in the back, threatened him and he left. I was still terrified that night when I left the lounge I could hardly drive for fear that he was following me and my girlfriend that had rode with me. I remained afraid for quite some time after that experience. I was so terrified about that incident that I would literally have dreams about that man. It also seemed like I always saw that man in the back of my mind. I was tormented and could not sleep for a long time.

When the police finally caught him, I was called down to the police station to identify him. It was him all right, but I was afraid to press charges because I did not want to look in his face. When they told me about his background and that he was from New York, just hearing that he was from New York made me even more afraid of him. Due to the fact that I was too afraid to press charges, they had to let him go, so I was always looking around thinking he was out there somewhere following me. Not only was I drinking alcohol, smoking reefer and snorting cocaine during this time in my life, I was also smoking angel dust and Sherman sticks, an elephant tranquilizer. Then I learned how to cook cocaine and started freebasing. I was now between twenty and twenty-one years old, I had my own car, a job and I was still shoplifting. One of my so-called friends introduced me to a big-time drug dealer in the city that began to give me anything I wanted. I would go home crying, asking my friends to pinch me so that I could see if how nice this man was treating me was real. It was like a fairy tale. He would buy me bottles of the elephant tranquilizer, mink coats, fur coats, jewelry and give me plenty of money. This went on for several months, then one day the phone rang and he began to tell me that the police were looking for him for murder. He wanted me to lie for him and say he was with me. Of course, that was out of the question. I was whacked out, but I was not that whacked out. I did like him a whole lot, because he was so nice to me before he had to start running from the police but I was not about to go to jail for perjury for him. I have never been a fool and I have never been slow. He had a baby momma, but I guess he did not want to jeopardize her life. Although the thought crossed my mind, I never asked him why didn't he ask his baby's momma to do it. I already knew why he didn't ask her to do it. Because he wanted to make sure if things didn't turn out right, she would be able to still be on the streets taking care of their child, while I would have been serving time in the penitentiary for perjury. I don't think so!

Well, several days later while I was sitting at home, he called me again and asked me to meet him down in the projects while he was still on the run from the police. I took my chances and went. I didn't know if he really wanted to see me because he cared about me, or if he wanted to hurt me because I wouldn't lie and say that we were together so that he could try to beat his case. After all, he had been taking good care of me by giving me any and everything he thought I wanted. I am sure he probably felt there should have been nothing that he asked me to do that I should not have been willing to do for him. When I arrived at the projects, his friends met me at my car and took me inside the project building. We went through a lot of dark hallways that smelled like urine that had not been cleaned for years. As we continued to walk through the dark, dreadful hallways, I was finally able to see my guy, my hero, who had tried to give me everything I had ever dreamed of. We hugged and kissed, talked for a while, then his friends escorted me back down to my car. Another drug dealer that I knew happened to be sitting in the parking lot on his car as I approached my car, and he said. "Little Jackie, Little Jackie, I have all pills and no money, please ask . . . . to let me sell my pills." It was not until that day that I found out I had been dating the man who was running the whole drug ring in the city of St. Louis, and not only was everybody afraid of him, but nobody could sell their drugs without his permission. Unbelievable!

God really watched over my life, because all my boyfriends were big-time drug dealers, gangsters and/or killers. The next day SWAT went in the projects and arrested my friend. I did not know I had been going with someone that notorious that they had to send SWAT in to get him. I had been in a dope house once before that had been raided with a prior boyfriend, but plain-clothes detectives came in on us, not SWAT. When the police kicked the dope house in, they took all of us that were in the drug house down to the police station, and then let us all go, except the guy I was going with at that time. I guess they had the one they were looking for.

On another occasion I rode to Winnipeg, Canada, with some of my other big-time drug-dealing friends who were like brothers to me. On our way back from Canada, after they had bought their drugs, and I am not talking about a small amount either, the police pulled us over for speeding. Thank God the officer didn't search the van that we were riding in because we all would have been facing hard time in the federal penitentiary.

Well, I still had my cocaine habit and I was still smoking Sherman sticks. I was beginning to hang out at the Voyager Lounge in St. Louis, where all the professional high-class working people, hustlers and notorious gangsters hung out. Because I was a top-flight booster I could out-dress any professional and fit in on any set. One day while at the Voyager Lounge, I met a nice schoolteacher. I went home with him and eventually started him on smoking Sherman sticks. We eventually started living together. He was really a nice, handsome, square, clean-cut guy. One day I had gotten ahold of some bad Sherman sticks and went on a bad drug trip that I had never been on before. I started hallucinating, and my friend started looking like Count Dracula with dark circles around his eyes, so I locked myself up in the bathroom and sat on the bathroom floor until he left for work. I then put on my mink coat that my other friend had given me that SWAT had locked up, and it had to be about 90 degrees outside.

Can you imagine that, a mink coat on in the summertime? The devil was trying to take my mind. I got in a taxi and told the driver to take me to my mother's house. When I got there I did not have a dime in my pocket to pay the taxi driver. I was so used to having money that I didn't realize I was broke, and I was so high I couldn't tell you if I had some money and left it or if I had no money at all. When my mother came out to the taxicab to get me, she was really worried about me. She wanted to admit me in a mental institution in St. Louis called Malcom Bliss, but when she called my father in Chicago and told him what was going on with me, he told her that whatever drug I had taken, it would wear off within forty-eight hours. He told her to send me up here to Chicago with him. I was about twenty-two years old then and I have been living here ever since.

I arrived at Chicago Midway Airport. It was a nice cool windy summer day. I had on a pair of hot pink velvet Gloria Vanderbilt pants with off-white stitching that had the name and symbol of Gloria Vanderbilt imprinted on them and an off white silk shirt, sharp as a tack and broke with nothing but a lot of pawn tickets in my luxurious, thick, leather, designer purse by Etienne Aigner, from pawning all of my jewelry. My hair was very thick and long. I was young, beautiful, and a nice size. My father owned a home and lived in one of those nice neighborhoods during those days that even had a miniature mansion on the same street that he lived on, which was on the far south side of Chicago, better known as the West Pullman area, south of the Roseland area here in Chicago.

Daddy didn't have the same lounge. He had a different lounge, and for some reason the one he had when I got here closed down after I was here for a while. Daddy also drove a Yellow cab in the daytime and ran his lounge at night on the nights it was open. Now here I am, a slick city girl from St. Louis, living in one of the squarest neighborhoods, I thought, on the south side of Chicago. I was broke and too afraid to use any of my boosting (shoplifting) skills because I was afraid that if I got locked up, they would lose me in the system, because I didn't know anything about the police system here in Chicago.

After my perm wore out of my hair and I didn't have any money to get it fixed, my hair started falling out, so I eventually had to end up getting it all cut off. I gained a lot of weight due to staying in the house all of the time, because I didn't know anybody. Therefore, I could no longer fit in any of those beautiful designer clothes that I moved here with, and every time I smoked a joint, I felt as if I had just smoked about three or four Sherman sticks. I felt border-line crazy, I was fat, ball headed and depressed, but this guy that lived around the corner from my father's house, who was not my type at all, was interested in me, so I would go over his house to visit because I didn't have anything else to do. He had two sisters; one of them was gay and the other one was straight. I would go over to their house and smoke up their reefers, drink up their alcoholic drinks and come back home and eat. I was getting fatter and fatter by the day and I was so miserable. I didn't like the new me at all. I couldn't imagine what that guy saw in me. And somehow he knew not to even try to ask me for a kiss or anything else, for that matter.

I later registered in a school called Roseland Community High School that was supposed to be an alternative high school where high school dropouts could go back to school and get their high school credits in order to graduate. That school was located in the portable buildings at Olive Harvey College, and because I thought I was slick, I pretty much talked the lady who was over the school into giving me my credits and letting me graduate. I did have a graduation and did receive a diploma, which I do not have a copy of now. And when I tried to call around to see if I could get a copy of a transcript or a copy of the diploma later, nobody seemed to know what happened to the school or the school records. Well, I didn't earn the diploma anyway, that is what I get. I talked the lady out of nothing, while I thought I was being so slick. When it came time for me to graduate from the school, my father did not even want to give me any money to get my hair done, but he eventually did.

I lived with my father, my stepmother, my stepsister, my stepsister's husband and their three children and my first cousin, the son of my father's baby sister, who died at the age of thirty-seven due to being a drug addict, prostitute and her organs shutting down, that I had just met for the first time. He was staying there with my father and my father was getting his social security check. I was told that somebody had given him something while he was away in college pledging in some fraternity that drove him crazy. He had to stay medicated all the time in order for him, or at least my father, to be able to keep getting his check. My cousin was very smart when he was not on that psychotropic medication that caused him to sleep all the time. He liked me a lot and was very happy that I was there. We would play chess together.

I considered myself to be a good chess player back then because I was about fourteen years old when I first learned how to play, but I could never win one game when I played against my cousin because he was really smart. I began to tell him to stop taking that medication because it made him look like a zombie. When he went to see his psychiatrist, he told him that I had told him to stop taking his medication, and my father asked me not to tell him not to take his medication anymore. My cousin would listen to me and he was beginning to look better when he had stopped taking that medication. I was tired of seeing him looking like a zombie and sleeping his life away when there was so much life and intelligence still left on the inside of him. Yes, I was a bad child, but I have always had a good heart.

My stepsister was not my father's child. However, he raised her and I am sure he took real good care of her when she graduated from high school. Here is that rejection thing again, which we will talk more about later. The spirit of rejection always made me feel like my stepmother was real mean toward me. I am going to leave out a lot of details concerning some of the things that I felt my stepmother was doing to me, because I have found out that when you often feel like people are being mean to you, they are usually telling you things that are going to be beneficial to you in life. I cherish and thank God for the things that my stepmother taught and instilled in me. I am nice to her now, because I can remember how my father was at the time. He was definitely not the type that I would ever say that I would want a man just like my father. With all honesty, I do not see how any woman would have put up with a man like him. My father wouldn't even give my stepmother money for extra groceries when I moved here. She would feed me with her food stamps. So I now remember the good things that she did, because she really didn't have to feed me. I was grown when I moved up here to Chicago. She didn't owe me anything and, realistically, at that age my father didn't either.

After living up here for a while, being depressed and broke, one of my neighbors came and told me that the Kool-Aid factory was hiring, because they were trying a new product called Crystal Light. I got up early that morning and stood in the line with hundreds of other candidates and I ended up getting the job. The job paid pretty good money too. My father immediately started charging me rent. Since I was free basing cocaine before I left St. Louis, I ended up starting off where I left off. And one of the reasons, or should I say excuses, was so that I could get some of that horrible weight off of me that I had gained. While working at the plant, one of the employees told me he had some good stuff and I bought some cocaine from him, took it home and cooked it. To my surprise, it was worth way more than I paid for it. The next time I bought some from him it was crap, so I started venturing out in the neighborhood. Crack cocaine has a spirit connected to it that will never allow you to be satisfied, so there I was chasing a rock every payday. One night I left the crack man's house and I didn't have any money left, but I still wanted to get high. As I approached the corner of our block, a nice-looking young brother stopped me in his car, a nice Cadillac, and offered me some money for sex. This man was so young and nice looking it was unbelievable. I actually thought he was going to try to hurt me or rob me. I took a chance and went with him anyway because that is how desperate a drug addiction will have you. He gave me the money and that was the beginning of sorrow. He had just taught me a new way to support my habit, since I was afraid of going boosting.

After a while the job laid those of us off that they had decided not to keep, and I was one of the ones that they let go, so I decided that I was not going to give my father any money out of my last check. He told me to either give him his rent or give him his key, so I chose to give him his key. I knew an older man who would let me live with him as I worked the streets to maintain my habit every day. Through hustling and getting high, I began to start meeting a lot of people. I also started learning about the spots to get the good stuff from. I would also meet new people from going in and out of jail for soliciting. When I first started out I was so beautiful and getting money was not a problem.

One night I was walking down the street hoping that somebody would stop and give me some money to get high. This young man that was driving a brand new Lincoln Town Car stopped. He asked me what was up, and I took him to my room where I was living. He gave me some money and

I ripped him off for the rest of his money and then told him to take me to the Lake Shore Drive Hotel where drugs were being sold. He took me and waited on me so that he could drive me back home. After we got on the expressway headed back to my place, he told me that his money was missing and that I had better give him his money. That was totally out of the question of course. As a crack addict, I couldn't give him any money back. I had already counted how many bags of cocaine I was going to buy with his money after he dropped me off. I was too crazy too give him his money back and I believe that caused the young man to like me even more. In addition, he felt sorry for me and told me he was going to come back the next day and buy me a television and some other things that I needed for the room I was renting. I just knew he was telling a lie.

The next day he came over in his Lincoln Town Car, dressed up in his business suit and took me shopping to buy the television and other accessories that he promised he was going to buy. Then he would come and visit me every day and buy my crack for me. One day he asked me to let him try it because he was tired of spending his money on it, and he wasn't getting anything out of it. I begged and pleaded with him and told him I would not give that to my worst enemy, but he thought I was just saying that because I wanted it all for myself, so he took it. He began to start smoking cocaine. He then ended up getting me an apartment and moving me out of the room I was renting. He let me keep his Lincoln Town Car because he had a college degree in engineering and he had to drive his company car to work. He also took me home to meet his mother because he really liked me.

I stopped going out on the streets and would only get high on his payday because I liked him a lot. His mother and I would hang out together every day, which kept me out of trouble, and she liked me a lot too. My soon to be mother-in-law only had seven boys and no girls, and my boyfriend was the oldest son. I also ended up being her first daughter-in-law. The whole family began to like me. I also ended up going to Dawson Skill Center, where I took up a trade so that I could become a Medical Transcriptionist. During the time I was in school, my half-brother and half-sister lived in the Ida B. Wells near 39th and Cottage Grove. My school had given me a grant check, so I would drive over to their house in my boyfriend's Lincoln Town Car that I drove to school in every day and get high. One morning at about 6:00 A.M., after getting high, I left my half-sister's house and went to get in the car, but the car was gone. I got afraid because I thought somebody had stolen his Lincoln Town Car. I got on the bus and went home.

When I arrived, the car was sitting out in front of our apartment. When I went upstairs and entered our apartment, he was very upset so he started arguing with me and hit me. I then called the police on him. When the police arrived at our apartment, my boyfriend began to tell the police that he had to go to school. He was a student at DePaul University. He was going to school to get his master's degree in Accounting in the evenings after working as an Engineer in the daytime. The police were getting ready to let him go to school and I got mad because I felt like the police should have locked him up for hitting me. Before I knew it I went to the refrigerator and took a big thick glass orange juice bottle out of the refrigerator that had water in it. As my boyfriend was walking across the room to get his jacket to go to school, I threw the bottle at him. The bottle met his head and busted it. It was unbelievable how that bottle met his head as he was walking to get his jacket so that he could go to school. I didn't know I could throw that good.

The police looked at me and told me I was going to jail now because I had busted his head right in front of them. They put the handcuffs on me, escorted me to the police car, pushed me in the car and off to jail I went. My boyfriend went to the hospital and got his head stitched up, and then went and borrowed the money to bond me out of jail. I was so happy to see him with a big red baseball cap on his head covering his bandages from the busted head I had just given him hours earlier.

We proceeded on with our lives as usual. After I graduated from my class, and had become a certified Medical Transcriptionist, I landed a job at St. Bernard Hospital as a billing clerk. My boyfriend and I would get paid and spend both our checks up on crack and would be broke by morning, but would be too tired to go to work, so we would both call off. We would then have to borrow money from his momma to buy food, and I would go to work without any lunch money, looking at everybody else at work eat their lunch. One day, a better job called me, so I gave the hospital a two-week notice that I was leaving and left the hospital to start my new job as a Senior Typist. After work, I would go and hang out at a lounge where all the bus drivers hung out. By then my relationship with my boyfriend was on the rocks, but he still allowed me to keep the car.

One day I decided that I was tired of spending all my money on crack cocaine. I was tired of getting paid one day and being broke the next. I had some friends that hung out at the lounge where I hung out that snorted heroin. They were more than happy to turn me on, because they knew I would end up becoming a heroin addict. I thought I was going to be able to leave the cocaine alone and just snort the heroin, but unfortunately I ended up with both habits. The guy that I was living with only smoked cocaine, and no matter how dope sick I got, he absolutely refused to buy me any heroin. I later ended up pregnant by him. We were still not getting along too well, so I asked him to drive me to St. Louis so that I could visit my mother for a while, and he did. Neither one of us knew that I was not supposed to travel during the first trimester of my pregnancy, and one day I started slightly bleeding, so I called him and he drove all the way back to St. Louis to pick me up. I started cramping so bad by the time we made it to Chicago that we went straight to Cook County Hospital, where we found out I was threatening a miscarriage. When his mother found out that I was pregnant, she told her son that he needed to marry me so that I would be able to get the medical care that I would need from the insurance he had on his job. So we got married. I later ended up losing the baby because of my addiction. It is sad to say, but I am glad that I did not bring a baby into this world at that time because I know I would have been an unfit mother.

As my addiction grew worse and worse, my relationship with my husband grew worse and worse. We ended up splitting up and I went back to working the streets again, smoking cocaine and snorting heroine on a greater level. Then one day there was a shortage of the heroin that I was snorting at that time called Karachi, so I started shooting dope. Before I knew it, I was shooting heroin and cocaine. I was living a real hard life. One night I met a lady they called black Betty and her boyfriend and she knew how to pick pockets real good. I knew that if it could be done I could do it too, so I learned how to pick pockets really good in order to support my habit, because I began to look so bad that when I could finally get someone to stop to give me some money to get high with, I could take everything they had. I could have gotten killed out there, but God spared my life. I ripped a lot of people off, and that is one thing people don't do and that is play around with is their money.

One night I got out of a man's car and he shot me in one of my buttocks. I never even went to the hospital to try to get the bullet out because I was too busy getting high. Another night a man talked me into going in the back of a bank, where he began to pistol whip me in my head. I heard a voice tell me to fall down and when I fell down the gunman ran. I struggled to get up and was able to make it to the main street, where a cab picked me up and took me to the hospital so that I could get my head stitched up in several places. If that man would have hit that soft spot in my head, I could have died.

One day I was trying to push a door open while I was angry and my arm went straight through the glass door and I cut an artery, some tendons and ligaments. While my arm was wrapped up, a lady asked me what happened to my arm and when I told her I cut an artery, she told me if I had cut an artery I could have died. One night a man picked me up in his car and I had ripped him off. As he was taking me back where he had picked me up at, instead of stopping to let me out where he should have, he started speeding real fast and I felt foul play, so I jumped out of his car. When I jumped out of the man's car, due to the shoes I had on, I slid up under the car and the car rolled over my ribs. I tried to get up off of the ground but I couldn't. When the ambulance arrived, they put me on a wooden board and rushed me to the hospital. When the doctor came in, he asked me what happened. I told him that a car had rolled over my ribs, and he told me if a car had rolled over me, I would have been smashed to death. I tried to raise myself up, and I asked him, "Don't you see the tire print?" After they took x-rays and saw my ribs were fractured, they admitted me in the hospital and kept me on morphine until my ribs finally healed. I have seen death so many times I have lost count, but God has kept me here.

Jail ended up becoming a revolving door for me. When I would end up in jail, the other inmates would look at me and say you didn't get arrested, you got rescued. This was very true, because every time I would go to jail, I would have an abscess on my body somewhere from shooting dope. If it had not gotten treated, that infection could have spread through my whole entire body, and I would have died. When I would go to jail I would go in looking horrible, but I would come out looking good. Although I would promise myself when I got out of jail I was not going to go back to getting high, each time it appeared that my addiction was getting worse and worse.

I remember one morning a man picked me up and looked at my profile and told me he could tell I *used* to be cute, and that really hurt my feelings. And to add to that, he didn't give me any money to get high with. If I'd had a pistol I would have stuck him up. My daddy even rode by me one day in his Yellow cab and told me I was just a wasted screw and that he wanted to shoot me and put me out of my misery. One day as I was high as a kite, the detectives pulled over and searched me and found a syringe and an empty bag of cocaine on me. They took me to jail and I was in there for six weeks. The detectives lied and said I had some cocaine on me. As strung out as I was, I knew for sure there was nothing in that bag for me to shoot, because it definitely would have been in me.

After the six weeks was up, and going back and forth to court as though I was some type of big-time drug dealer, the judge finally gave me two years' probation, which meant that if I got locked up for anything within that time frame, I would have to go to the penitentiary and serve my time. Due to having a bad habit that had to be fed, I still had to do what I had to do in order to get my fix every day, in spite of what the judge said. I didn't know that drugs was not a natural problem back then. It was a spiritual problem, but I did remember my grandmother always telling me to call on Jesus to help me whenever I was in any kind of trouble. I was able to stay on the streets for a long time, using drugs to live and living to use drugs.

I remember how I used to take over the Kentucky Fried Chicken's bathroom on 119th and State Street to shoot my dope. One day I was in their bathroom shooting some heroin and cocaine mixed together, which is called a speedball, and something supernaturally knocked the needle out of my leg. I know if any more would have gotten in my system, I would have died from an overdose right there in that bathroom. At that time I was so burnt up that I had been shooting dope all in my arms, neck, feet, hands and legs. I didn't have any more veins to go in. I would get so high that I couldn't get high anymore. I would smoke so much cocaine till my hands would start shaking so bad that I couldn't hold the cocaine pipe. I would shoot or snort some heroine in order to come down off the cocaine. I was pitiful, in very bad shape. Sometimes I would smoke the cocaine pipe and shoot dope, and other times I would mix the cocaine and heroin together and shoot it.

One day, after I had gotten so high, and I still had drugs and money left, I decided that I would just go outside and make some more money. As I was walking down the street, I began to cry out, "Help me Jesus, help me Jesus, help me!" from the top of my lungs. I somehow knew that Jesus was the only answer for me. When the Lord really started dealing with me, it seemed like whenever I got dope sick, I would go where I was living at the time, with a nice man who took care of me during my addiction, and turn on the Christian television station. One day as I was flicking through the channels, I began watching Pastor Richard D. Henton from the Monument of Faith Church. He was preaching a message called "Get off the Hell Bound Train." As he was preaching, I held my poor little weak arm up in the air, which was so weak due to me being dope sick. I was going through the motions, as if I was pulling the cord on a bus that you would pull to let the driver know to let you off at the next stop. I even called their prayer line that night and the person on the other end of the phone tried to convince me to come to the church. But I can also remember the devil telling me not to go to church because the people were going to laugh at me because of my attire. All I had at that time were clothes a hooker would wear. So I continued on with the lifestyle that I was living, but yet calling on God for help. Although during this time I had a nice place where I could go and stay, I was getting so high and tired that I was sleeping in cars, on top of a friend's pool table in his game room, or on the floor in a shooting gallery. A lot of people were very nice to me out there during my addiction that I will never forget.

I can remember a time I was so high off of heroin on a very hot summer day that I had my head hanging out of this young man's car. A lady in another car hollered over to the driver and asked him if I was all right. He replied, "She just needs Jesus." The lady asked him to pull his car over, and she began to witness to me and asked me to go home with her so that she could take me to church that night. I climbed into her car and went with her to her home. I can remember after taking a bath, she gave me this yellow and black outfit to put on that was so big on me it could have wrapped around me twice, so she had to pin it up on me. I can remember her telling me that she was getting ready to take me to her church, but she said the Lord had spoken to her and told her to take me to Monument of Faith Church. When she took me there, I believe it was on a Friday, Apostle Henton was not there. I remember some people praying for me but nothing happened. The lady who had taken me to the church called Haymarket House drug rehab to see if they had a bed for me. They told her yes, but due to me having a heroin habit, I needed to go to Cook County Hospital and get a doctor's statement saying I was healthy enough to be admitted in their facility. The lady took me to the hospital to get the documentation that was requested and then Haymarket House came to pick me up from the hospital. I stayed in their program for about three days but left because my addiction was calling me.

Since I knew how to pick pockets so well, dope fiends, although they can be very scandalous people, would be real nice to me because they knew I was always going to have some money or be on my way to get some money. I had one friend who worked in the dope house that would always let me in because he wanted to get high off of my drugs with me. We all know that money talks, and I got so much money out there on the streets that if I was the only customer a dope man had, he made him some good money on a good day. One day I was getting ready to go home, but I had picked a pocket and had gotten well over five hundred dollars. For some reason, I didn't want to go home and get high by myself, so my friend who worked at the dope house was getting off from work. We called working at the dope house a job, and we went over to some other associates house. I can remember taking one shot of dope, and when I woke up they had stolen all of my drugs and money. Because of how bad my habit was, I woke up very dope sick and nobody would even give me any dope to get my sick off. Not even my so-called friend that I went over there with who worked at the dope house.

When I made it back to the neighborhood where I would hustle, my friend was at the dope house working. I just so happened to pick a pocket and had gotten over a thousand dollars. I knocked on the door of the dope house and told my so-called friend to open the door and let me in. He wouldn't open the door because he thought I didn't have any money and that I wanted to get in to beg him for whatever little drugs he was making for working there. When I started passing hundred dollar bills through the hole in the door, telling him how many bags of heroin to give me; and how many bags of cocaine to give me, he told me to come around to the front door so that he could let me in the house. I told him no thanks. It is all right now. I know he was sick, because after he gave me the drugs I had paid for, I flashed the rest of the hundred dollar bills I had in his face and left.

One night after getting high for a couple of nights straight, the police finally pulled me over and told me to get in the car. They told me I was soliciting, and I tried my best to convince them that I wasn't, because I knew I was on probation. I knew I was supposed to have to serve 2 years due to being on probation if I got caught doing anything. After we got to the police station and the police took my fingerprints, they put me in a prison cell. Because I knew I wouldn't be getting out anytime soon, and that I was going to be transferred to Cook County Jail, I lied and told the police that my chest was hurting. Due to all of the experience I had gotten from going back and forth to jail, I knew that if you told the police your chest was hurting, they had to take you to the hospital. I really just wanted to go to the hospital so that I could try to get some candy from somebody, because all drug addicts like sweets, especially if they can't get a fix.

On our way to the hospital, the police officers decided they wanted some White Castle hamburgers, so I was able to get a burger. That was very unusual to get a hamburger from a police officer. Once we made it to the hospital and I explained to the nurse that my chest was hurting, they immediately waited on me. Once the doctor ran tests, he said that he did find something wrong with my heart and that he was going to have to admit me. That was really a surprise to me because I only lied to get to the hospital to get some candy. When the nurse tried to find a vein to put the IV in my arm, she saw that I didn't have any good veins anymore. They were all burned out from me shooting drugs. Then the doctor came over to try to find a vein, and because I didn't have any, he decided to make an incision in my left thigh to run an IV in me. When that happened it looked like my life flashed before my face; and I realized that if I had gotten hurt on the streets and they would not have been able to put an IV in me in time I could have died, so I began to cry and call on Jesus. That made one of the police officers very mad. She said, "That just kills me that every time they get in trouble they want to start calling on Jesus." I didn't care what she was saying. I was serious. After the procedure was done with the IV, they took me to my room and handcuffed me to the bed-as if I was really some hard-core criminal who had committed a murder or something.

As I lay there in the hospital, the police were continually changing shifts. I had been in the hospital for about three days. The night before Cook County Jail came to pick me up, when the shift changed, a lady police officer who was saved, a born-again Christian was assigned to me and she asked me if I had ever thought about being saved. I looked up at her and told her, "Ma'am, even Jesus don't want me. Her comment to me was, "Baby, wherever there is still life there is still hope." Those words that came out of her mouth really stuck with me. She helped me realize that God was keeping me around for a reason. Yet due to my addiction, because I knew she was a nice saved lady, I continually asked her for candy and sandwiches. She gave them to me, as much as I wanted, but most of all she gave me hope! After her shift ended, Cook County Jail was there to pick me up. I got dressed and was transported to Cook County Jail. Once we arrived at the jail, they processed me and told me that my court date was not going to be until February and then they took me to my tier. While I was in jail I happened to pick up a book that said if I consistently prayed, something would happen. So I did keep praying as best I knew how for God to help me. Then because the jail was over crowded, many of us had to sleep on the floor in the dayroom. That is when I met this backslidden Sunday school teacher. We did like most sinners. We talked about Jesus for a while and then we talked about drugs for a while.

Mind you, my court day was not supposed to be until February and my backslidden Sunday school teacher friend's court date happened to be January 23, 1992. On that day the guard came and told me to get ready for court. I told the guard it was not my court date and that she needed to go check her paperwork, because I did not feel like lying around in the bull pen all day at one of those small jails for nothing. The guard was so sweet and humble, so she nicely went to check her paperwork and came back to me and told me to get ready for court. Once my friend saw that I was going to court too, she told me that if we had gotten out together that I could go home with her and she would get me high, so I was definitely going to follow her if we got out together. When I got to the courthouse, the public defender who was assigned to my case told me that because I was on probation I needed to see my probation judge and to ask for a continuance on the soliciting charge I was going before the judge for. I did just the opposite. When I went before the judge, I pleaded guilty to the soliciting charge and the judge gave me time considered served. When I got back to the big jail and my backslidden friend got back, she said that she was going home that night. I told her that I was probably going to have to stay in jail to go see my probation judge. However, the strangest thing happened that night. The guards called me to be discharged to go home, but they did not call my friend to be discharged. I didn't realize that God was separating me from my backslidden Sunday school teacher friend.

That day the weather was very strange. It was very nice when we went to court that morning, but when the guards were escorting me out of the jail, they asked me where my coat was. I told them it was in my bag, so they told me I had better put it on. When I got outside it was the worse blizzard I had ever seen. I couldn't believe it. However, that didn't matter because the weather had never stopped me from getting money and drugs in the past. But this time the weather was so bad that there wasn't a soul out there, so I went on home to the man's house that I was living with at the time. When I knocked on the door, he answered and said, "I shouldn't let you in." I explained to him that I had been in jail, so he opened the door and let me in. He told me to go in the back and sleep in the extra bedroom in the house, as if he really did not want to have anything to do with me anymore. He had never reacted like that before.

This guy had literally taken care of me during my addiction and I had taken him through the ringer. My addiction was so bad that I would be gone for days at a time. He bought my clothes, my food and provided a place for me to live in spite of my lifestyle. He had never refused to let me in before. Well, I went on in the back room and went to sleep as he suggested. I couldn't believe that he didn't want me to sleep in our bedroom either, but I was just glad to get in, so I didn't ask any questions. When I woke up the next morning, he was gone to work, so I turned the radio on a gospel station. A lady on the radio was singing a song that said, "I complained that I have no shoes, when there is a man that has no feet to use." At that time, my whole life flashed before my face and I thought about how I still had arms. All of a sudden my arms flew up in the air and I began to say, "I am out of the darkness into the light." Of course I didn't know what that meant, and then I began to say, "I don't have to do drugs anymore." As I was saying those things, I was doing the Holy Ghost dance that I had never done before in my whole entire life,.

When I stopped, I immediately called my mother in St. Louis and shared with her what had just happened to me, but she thought I was just on a bad drug trip. When I hung up from talking to my mother, I called the backslidden Sunday school teacher's house that I had met in jail, and her mother answered the phone. I told her that I was in jail with her daughter and asked her if her daughter had made it home, and she said no. I then began to tell her about the spiritual experience that I had just had, and I told her that I was scared. She told me, "Baby, don't be scared. The Lord has just set you free." When I got off the phone I had to go in the bathroom to throw up. God was purging me then, but of course I still didn't have a clue about what was going on with me. Then I was led to call Monument of Faith Church, where that lady had taken me that night. A lady answered the phone and told me that they had prayer service there at the church at 9:00 a.m. on Mondays, Tuesdays, Wednesdays and Fridays, and at noon on Thursdays. I decided to go to the noon service on Thursday, because I was not a morning person. Especially after all of those years I had spent in darkness. When I arrived at the church, the lady in the bookstore gave me my first brand-new Bible. Of course, I didn't know that God speaks to His children and tells them to bless other people. She then walked me to the prayer room where all of the prayer warriors were on their knees speaking in tongues. I was ready to leave because I didn't understand a word they were saying, but the lady encouraged me to stay. She told me that they would be finished praying shortly.

As I sat there, the lady leading the Thursday prayer meeting, who was Mother Akins at the time, began to speak. After her sermon she asked if anybody had a testimony. Before I knew it my arm flew up and I said, "I do." Then I thought about what I had done, because I was not a bold person who would ever speak in front of a crowd, I immediately got nervous. Mother Akins began to call on some of the other saints that had a testimony before she got to me, and of course I was glad she didn't call me. As a matter of fact, I was really praying that she would just forget that my arm flew up in the first place, and that "I do" had flown out of my mouth because that was definitely not me who said that. Well, she didn't forget about me. She told me to stand up to tell my testimony, and so I nervously stood up and said, "I am so glad my Jesus didn't forget about me," and before I knew it, I began to stump on the floor saying how the devil couldn't hurt me no more. I was just a preaching telling my testimony about how the Lord had delivered me from drugs, until I finally fell down on the floor. I was spiritually drunk before I left that service.

When it was time for us to leave that day, one of the other

mothers started asking me where I lived. I told her with my boyfriend because I didn't know any better. She then told me, "Whatever you do, don't you sleep with that man." Then another lady named Mother Lenora Hollister told me that the Lord had told her to take care of me, so she took me home. When I went home from prayer, I was in the back room, where my boyfriend had suggested I sleep, reading my Bible. Of course, here comes the test. He asked me to have sex with him and I told him that I couldn't because I was saved now. He said, "What you mean . . . I have been taking care of you all this time." I told him, "But Jesus took me off drugs." He didn't like that but I didn't care. Although I was a baby Christian, it was as if I heard Jesus tell me that if I stayed with my boyfriend and continued to have sex with him, the drug addiction would come with it, but if I moved and was obedient to Him (Jesus) I would remain free.

Later that night my boyfriend started an argument with me and even tried to swing on me. That was not him. That was the devil, because all during my addiction, this man had never been anything but very nice and sweet to me. He was not the type of man that would hit a woman. He was a very hard-working man who grew up in the south. He worked for the City of Chicago, out in the cold in the winter and in the hot scorching sun in the summertime, on the train rails as an ironworker.

Of course, at that time I didn't know that darkness and light would always clash. I can remember those words so vividly when I received that visitation from the Lord. He spoke through me and said I am out of the darkness and into the light. Now that I have matured in God, I know that the Scripture says, "What concord has darkness with light?" This is why God told us to come out from amongst them.

He knew that Cain would try to kill Abel and that Joseph's brothers would never have the ability to speak peaceably with him because of the light he was walking in and the anointing on his life. The coat of many colors that Joseph's father gave him represented the anointing that was on his life. Not to mention, Joseph always reminded his evil, jealous brothers that he was the chosen one. I believe that my friend did not know what he was doing when he swung on me. The devil knew that I had transitioned from darkness to light, so he entered into my friend's body and he had it in for me. I called Mother Hollister, who had told me that God had told her to take care of me. She came right over, but because she was a married woman she advised me to go on back home and that we would make plans on what I was going to do the next day.

The next day she asked a single lady who was saved, but spiritually immature, if I could come and stay with her. The lady told her it was fine for me to come. She lived in a studio apartment, and I had to sleep on the floor on an air bag, which was fine with me because I always remembered the Words that the Lord had spoken to me. He said if I stayed in the house with the man that I was living with, the drugs would come with it, but if I was obedient and went where He told me to go, I would have the ability to stay free. Well of course when you first move into a place, it appears that everything is going to work out just fine. But Mother Hollister had already told me that the Lord was going to work on my life as well as the lady that I moved in with, meaning that God was going to begin to show us ourselves, and if we allowed Him to He was going to take those things out of us that would cause us to be a reproach to the gospel and put those things in us that would cause us to be those walking epistles read of men so that we could bring glory to Him. Well, the lady and I had good days and bad days, then before I knew it the demons began to manifest through her in such a way that I did not feel welcome there anymore. During those days of my new born-again Christian life, many difficult tests came my way. I passed some and failed others.

I was so used to going to the crack house to use drugs and back to the streets to get more money to get high with. Now I was saved and I absolutely didn't know what to do with myself. I would sit there in the studio apartment with earplugs in my ears listening to gospel music all day. When I would go to the church services, the pastor who laid my foundation, Pastor Richard Daniel Henton, was very funny to me. I never knew I could laugh so much without smoking a joint. Since I felt so unwelcome at the studio apartment that I was living in, I would go to the 8:00 a.m. service, Sunday School at 10:00, wait for the 2:30 p.m. service to start, and enjoy that service, then go to the lunch room and eat and stay for the 7:00 p.m. Broadcast service. The devil meant it for evil, but God brought good out of it. Since I felt unwelcomed in the apartment, I stayed at all those services and was able to get a whole lot of Word. I was growing and witnessing, telling people about the goodness of Jesus everywhere I went.

One day I ran into a lady who had ministered to me when I was not saved and she told me that she was living on the West Side of Chicago. She gave me her phone number and I called her the next day. When she answered the phone, she invited me over. When I arrived at the house that she was living in, I discovered that she was living there with an older couple. Of course I didn't pry into her business, but I guessed that she was possibly renting a room from the couple. Well, when I met the older couple I had the ability to see the condition the house was in on the floor where the older couple was living. The older lady asked me to come back the next day and clean up for them. I returned the next day and cleaned the house up real good for them. I had worked tiringly hard that day and when it was time for me to go home, I was not even offered fifty cents to buy a cold pop. Well, I got on the bus and began to read this book that I was reading by Morris Cerullo. A man got on the bus who did not have enough money to pay his bus fare. He asked the whole bus if anyone had seventy-five cents. I reached in my pocket and said, "Sir, here is fifty-five cents." The man came to the back of the bus where I was sitting and said, "Out of this whole bus wouldn't anybody give me seventy-five cents. You see this fifty-dollar bill. It is real here, ma'am." I believe that I had entertained an angel unaware that day. I believe the Lord was paying me for cleaning up those elderly people's house who probably could not afford to pay me.

I continued to go over to the elderly couple's house and eventually moved in with them. During that time, I was up against a lot of opposition because we must all realize that although we might be baby Christians, the devil knows who we are. The devil was doing everything he could to try to run me away from Christianity and the Lord allowed him to do everything that he was doing. Because of how aggressively the devil was coming after me, I believe it caused God to open up my spiritual eyes immediately. We have spiritual eyes and natural eyes. With our spiritual eyes we have the ability to see in the spirit and see visions. We have a spiritual nose and a natural nose. With our spiritual nose we have the ability to smell sin and sickness. We also have spiritual ears and natural ears. With our spiritual ears we have the ability to hear the voice of the Lord and things that are going on in the spirit realm. Remember in *II Kings 6:12* how the prophet Elisha had the ability to hear what was going on in the king's bed chamber, which caused the king to be very angry. We have to realize that the enemy loves to keep us carnal and without knowledge. He does not want us to know that we have the ability to see, smell and hear in the Spirit. Our ability to hear, smell and see in the spirit causes us to have the ability to maneuver around danger. Therefore, the enemy tries to stop up our spiritual ears and blind our spiritual eyes.

> *Ezekiel 12:2*
> *Son of man, thou dwellest in the midst of a rebellious house, which have eyes to see, and see not; they have ears to hear, and hear not: for they are a rebellious house.*

> *Matthew 13:15–16*
> *For this people's heart is waxed gross, and their ears are dull of hearing, and their eyes they have closed; lest at any time they should see with their eyes and hear with their ears, and should understand with their heart, and should be converted, and I should heal them.*

> *But blessed are your eyes, for they see: and your ears, for they hear.*

As we see in Ezekiel 12:2, rebellion is the reason the house of Israel had eyes to see and could not see and ears to hear and could not hear. It is important for us to deal with every area of rebellion in our lives so that we will have the ability to defeat the enemy. When a person is walking in darkness, they do not have the ability to see like people that are walking in the light. In addition, the enemy is the ruler of darkness, so when there is any kind of darkness in our lives, this gives him the ability to rule us. This is the season we have to allow the Word of the Lord to have free course in our lives. Even Jesus said He was not going to talk much, because once the prince of this world, (the devil) came, He wouldn't have anything on the inside of Him. The church is getting ready to arise to another dimension. We are going to let our yea be yea and our nay be nay. God is going to bridle our tongues. There is a purification taking place on the inside of many of us and we are not going to compromise or play with the enemy because of the anointing that God has placed in our lives.

Many of us are also going to sell all the way out in this season as painful as it may tend to be to our flesh. There are some people that we are going to still love, speak to and honor, but we are not going to be able to hang out with them because of the love they still have for the things of the world. People who honor the anointing on your life are not going to just feel comfortable cursing and saying all types of things around you. We have got to guard our own hearts because that is where words are sown. We all have some sort of idea of what we can listen to and what we can't listen to. Do not be so hard up that you have to be in the presence of people who are being used by the devil to water down the anointing that God has placed on your life. You can't do what others can do. When there is something that someone else is doing that you cannot do, don't just do it to be accepted by that person. They may be able to do it and get away with it, but it might make you backslide. We all come from different walks of life. I know that due to the depth of sin that I came from, I cannot do certain things, go certain places, or listen to certain things. I do not condemn those who can, but I have to work out my own salvation.

Some of us have to learn obedience by the things that we suffer (Hebrews 5:8). One day I was on the bus and I began to talk to this young man. Due to the impartations that I had received, God would use me prophetically. While I was ministering to this man that I had no business ministering to in the first place, he was very receptive and even started going to church with me. The reason I said I did not have any business ministering to the young man is because before I got saved, all of my friends were men, but God was trying to change that about me because He wanted me to witness to women. In His wisdom, He knew the traps that the enemy was going to try to set for me. Well, the young man was attracted to me and he was not a bad-looking guy. As a matter of fact, he was very handsome. He had also gotten saved, or at least he was going to church, possibly pretending to be saved so that he could try to marry me. However, I am not in a place that I can judge rather he was saved or not.

Anyway, we had started spending a lot of time together every day. I had not been saved for more than two years myself and of course I would have preferred to hang out with a man instead of a woman. Well, my man friend and I would go everywhere together and we had a very clean relationship. He honored me as a woman of God, his mentor and the one who had led him to the Lord. In spite of the attraction that he felt for me, he remained respectful. Then one day he brought his niece over to my house, and she was only six years old. He knew what he was doing because I did not have any children due to a miscarriage I had when I was addicted to drugs.

I began to be very crazy about his niece, who is still my favorite niece today, because her uncle and I did end up getting married. But before we got married we fell into fornication one time, and I felt as if my entire relationship with the Lord had totally fallen apart. Things got suddenly dark and I just couldn't see my way. God used the man with whom I had fornicated with to encourage me to go to church that next morning and I am so glad I did. Otherwise, I would not be writing this book today. At that time I did not know the Lord as Father. I only knew him as Savior and Lord. The reason I ended up falling into fornication is because I never had any business being alone with male company to begin with, because the Bible tells us not to let our good be evil spoken of. Furthermore, I was not divorced from the man that I had married before I had gotten saved, who had about thirteen children by another woman. On top of that, I had to wait until we were legally divorced before I could marry the guy who was so willing to marry me.

As soon as I received my divorce papers; this guy and I, with whom I had fallen into fornication with, got married. He was a very good hard-working man that believed in taking care of me, his wife. Unfortunately, one day he backslid and after that he kept perpetually backsliding. He began to get violent and I eventually had to leave him after trying my best to hang in there with him. After I separated from him, I had to leave Monument of Faith Church because I knew as long as we stayed at the same church, I never would have developed enough strength to leave him and would remain in the same situation because I really loved my husband, whom the devil had entered in to try to hinder me from fulfilling my destiny. I needed a lot of healing and deliverance after leaving him, because one minute I would think about all the good things he had done and the next minute I would be thinking about all of the painful things he had done to me. I felt like a basket case. I would be working and tears would just roll down my face, because now I had to walk alone, without my husband.

Since I had to leave Monument of Faith in order to remain

free from my husband, the Lord sent me to Crusaders Church, where Apostle John Eckhardt is the Apostle and Senior Pastor. What the devil means for evil, the Lord will always bring good out of it. I began to learn a whole lot more about the prophetic and deliverance, and I took every class they were offering at the time. Apostle Eckhardt has such a strong grace on his life to launch people into ministry that before I knew it, I had opened up my first homeless shelter. I am now the founder and overseer over two homeless shelters that consist of 120 beds and a ministry. In spite of my background, God made me an entrepreneur and a preacher. I have been saved for twenty-four years now, and I love the Lord. The knowledge, lessons and things I experienced as a drug addict have enabled me to do the work that I do with love and compassion. I know firsthand how it feels to be a drug addict and I also know firsthand how it feels to be a born-again Christian. I would not trade the life I live now for anything in the world. The Lord has restored the years of my life that were stolen through drugs and addiction.

In order to stay off drugs, we must continue to stay focused and seek first the kingdom of God and His righteousness and allow Him to add everything else unto us.

Four

THE POWER OF KNOWING OUR PURPOSE

Jeremiah 1:5
Before I formed thee in the belly I knew thee; and before thou camest forth out of the womb I sanctified thee, and I ordained thee a prophet unto the nations.

Before God forms us in the belly of our mother, He already knows who we are and what He has called us to do. We were created by design. There is only one you and there will never be another you. We were fearfully and wonderfully made. Jeremiah 1:5 also says that before the prophet Jeremiah came out of his mother's womb, God had already sanctified him. That word *sanctified* means "to be set apart for a sacred and particular purpose." We all have a purpose and we need to know what our purpose is. Our purpose is simply our reason for existing; the reason we were born. If you don't know what your purpose is, ask God what your purpose is. We have a better advantage in life when we know what our purpose is. Knowing our purpose will help us get headed in the right direction and keep us from fainting along the way. In spite of the different situations or circumstances we end up in we will still have a gut feeling that things are not going to be the way they are always.

Also in Jeremiah 1:5, we see that God had already ordained Jeremiah a prophet unto the nations. As we looked up the word *ordained* we found that some of its synonyms mean "intended, predestined, destined, preordained, appointed and predetermined." You have already been ordained to be who you are. I am not talking about who you may be acting like right now if you are battling with any type of an addiction or sin. I am talking about who God created you to be. I mean the finished work, when the Lord is finished transforming your life by the power of the Holy Spirit. I am so grateful that God had already predetermined that He would not allow me to die in my addiction. God already knew before he formed me in my mother's belly what He had predestined for me to do. I just didn't know what the Lord's purpose for me was because the devil had made my life so dark and gloomy. I can even remember having thoughts of suicide as a child. I believe if I had owned a gun, I would have ended my own life way before I had ever gotten strung out on drugs. Lastly, in Jeremiah 1:5 we see that God had ordained the prophet Jeremiah to be a prophet unto the nations. The nations were his sphere of influence. Know that there are places that the Lord will send us to, and a certain sector of people that He will send us to minister to, so that we can be influential and instrumental in their lives.

When I was having suicidal thoughts early in my childhood, I had no idea that it was the devil putting those thoughts in my mind, wishing I would carry them out so that I would not be here today fulfilling my destiny. God didn't place us on the earth to do what the devil tells us to do. He placed us on the earth so that we can tell the devil what to do. God created all of us in His image and likeness. We are supposed to look and operate like God. He created all of us to rule the earth. He created all of us for His glory and His pleasure, but we all have different assignments. Assignments are tasks, projects, jobs, and obligations. Your assignments will help you fulfill your purpose. You cannot fulfill your purpose or destiny without knowing who you are. God is a ruler and He created us to rule the earth. Marijuana, heroin and cocaine are plants that grow out of the earth. We are supposed to rule the earth and not allow the earth to rule us. Once you come to the realization of who you are and Who you have living on the inside of you, you will no longer bow down to a plant. Drugs will no longer run your life and tell you what to do.

All spirits have a voice, and drugs have a voice; they tell us what to do to get them, where to get them, and how much to get. When you begin to walk in authority, when you begin to rule as God intended, you will tell the spirit of drugs to shut up. God has given us power over all of the power of the enemy. Drugs are our enemy when we use them frivolously ourselves. The only time any type of drug should be used is if it is prescribed legally by a doctor or as an anesthesia for surgery. So many doctors write prescription drugs with codeine and other substances in them in order to keep people as their patients. Be very careful if you have been on street drugs so that you do not become addicted to prescription drugs. I have been saved for over twenty-four years and the devil still tries to tempt me with drugs. I just know who I am today, I know my purpose and I know the Lord paid a great price for my salvation. I also love the Lord so much and I am grateful that He set me free. When you begin to love the Lord and develop a relationship with Him, you will no longer want to do anything to hurt Him. The love you have for the Lord will also help you fulfill your purpose. The Bible lets us know that if we submit to the Lord and resist the devil he will flee.

Adam's assignment was to dress and care for the Garden of

Eden. When God told Adam to care for the garden, Adam was supposed to make sure the garden was tilled, watered, cultivated and that it had everything it needed in order to grow. God wanted everything that He made that was good to be fruitful and multiply. Adam was also told to keep the garden, which means he was supposed to protect and guard the garden. Anytime we are told to guard something, that automatically means it is our job to keep all intruders out. Next, God sealed his instructions in Adam, telling him that he could eat from every tree of the garden except from the tree of the knowledge of good and evil. God was setting boundaries, restrictions, limitations and borderlines for Adam. Once we pass boundaries that have been set for our lives, we are trespassing. Going places that have been prohibited and forbidden by the Lord is always an act of rebellion. Acts of rebellion will always get us in trouble. Another thing I would like to point out concerning God telling Adam not to eat from the tree of the knowledge of good and evil is that we are a product of whatever we eat. God did not want Adam to know how to be good and evil. He only wanted Adam to be good and innocent. This is why God told Adam that the day that he ate of the tree of the knowledge of good and evil, he was going to end up spiritually dead, backslidden. After God gave Adam his assignment and sealed His instructions on the inside of him, God decided to give Adam a help-mate because He felt it was not good for Adam to be alone.

However, an intruder, the devil in the form of a serpent, ends up invading the garden and convinces Adam's wife, Eve, to eat from the tree of the knowledge of good and evil, and she gave to Adam, her husband, and he did eat. After Adam ate from the tree, his innocence was immediately taken from him and his wife, and they realized they were naked. Due to their act of disobedience, they were kicked out of the Garden of Eden. However, Jesus came to redeem mankind and give us back everything that Adam had lost. Therefore, when we fail at fulfilling our assignment, because of the blood of Jesus that He shed on Calvary for our sins, we have another opportunity to fulfill that which we failed to do the first time we were told. We have got to understand that regardless of past mistakes, how things look in our lives right now, regardless of what we are going through, God will give us another chance to do things right and He has a better plan for our lives. I had to believe, that in spite of the addiction that I was battling, God was not going to leave me in the situation that I was in and that He not only had the ability to forgive me, but He desired to change, transform and help me. The Bible tells us that Jesus came to destroy the works of the devil, so this allows us to know that He wants to destroy every devil that is working and operating in our lives.

The majority of people who battle any type of addiction think they are nickel dime slick because once an addiction really gets bad, an addict has to have some type of hustle in order to support their habit. As an addiction gets worse, working a 9:00 A.M. to 5:00 P.M. job is not enough money to support a real drug habit. Jeremiah 31:11 says that the Lord has redeemed Jacob. Jacob's name means "trickster." Redeemed means "to liberate free or convert." This scripture also says that He ransomed Jacob from the hand of him who was too strong for him. We cannot change, convert, transform, or give ourselves a born-again experience. Only the Lord can do that, because without the Lord Jesus, drugs are stronger than us. After the Lord comes on the inside of our lives, then we are stronger than the drugs, because greater is He who is in us than he that is in the world.

I have noticed that some people in the church are still using drugs. Before I got saved, delivered, converted, liberated and set free from drugs, my whole day consisted of going out on the streets to make money to support my drug habit, then back to the dope house to buy more drugs to get high. I did that repetitiously every day for over eleven years, so once the Lord delivered me from the drugs, I did not know what to do with myself. We have to ask God to allow our mind to comprehend what has taken place in our spirit, because if our mind does not comprehend what has taken place in our spirit, we will still be trying to get high, because that is all we know and have been doing for a long period of time.

Once we have been born again, we have to learn how to live the new life that the Lord has given us. First of all, you must know (comprehend) that you are not the old person you used to be. Unless you come to this realization, you will keep perpetually backsliding. I really don't want to get ahead of myself in this book, but in order for me to get a point across, I have to tell you that after the Lord saved me and grew me up spiritually, He allowed me to open up several homeless shelters. Yes, He transformed a dope fiend into a preacher and entrepreneur.

Anyway, it was a guy that I knew way before I had opened my first shelter that was at another shelter that I used to minister at that ended up coming to one of the shelters that the Lord had allowed me to open, because the shelter he was living in had closed down. After we did an intake on him, we placed him in the back room of the house which was going to be his sleeping area. He would be back in his room praying real loud and good, and the whole shelter could hear him. He could pray so good that he could have fooled the very elect, but we found out later that he was back their getting high off of crack cocaine while he was doing all of that loud praying. Do not allow that to be you. Do not put up a façade. Please get the deliverance that you need, because that is a dangerous place that young man was in or could possibly still be in. We bring curses upon ourselves when we pretend to be somebody we are not in order to receive the praises of men. Gifts and callings are without repentance. A gift will work as long as you stir it up. Paul told his spiritual son Timothy to stir up the gift that was in him that was given him by the laying on of his hands. But Jesus told us that a tree is known by the fruit it bears and for us to either make the tree good or make it evil.

One day when I was getting ready to go preach at the shelter I was preaching at before the Lord allowed me to open ours, I had gotten into a confrontation, and I had cursed and pulled a knife out on someone. I had only been saved for a little over two years and I had no idea those spirits were still in me. After I got finished allowing the devil to make a fool out of me, I immediately fell down on my knees and told the Lord that the people that I was going to minister to might as well minister to one another. I called the shelter and let them know that I would not be there that day and asked the leader of the home if she would speak in my place. Of course I didn't tell them why! I had also made a list of the women in the home that I was going to allow to speak until the Lord delivered me, but the Lord delivered me that night, so I was able to take my rightful place back in the ministry the following week. Sometimes, you have to let the Lord know that you thank Him for the gift that He has blessed you with, but you would prefer His character much more than the gift. Sometimes, we have to place a demand on the Lord. I told Him that I refused to preach in the state that I was in, and He did something about it. I am not saying sit down in ministry every time you make a mistake, but I am saying don't get comfortable giving the Lord any kind of sacrifice.

If we continue sinning and preaching, our conscience will get seared with a hot iron, which means we will not get convicted when we are doing wrong anymore. We must confess our sins to the Lord so that He will forgive us and cleanse us from all unrighteousness. The difference between us, the true men and women of God, and the devil is that the devil can preach the Word of God, but he can't live it. We, the children of God, are supposed to make our bodies a living sacrifice to the Lord.

Also, when we are battling any type of an addiction, the devil would like for us to believe that there is no hope for us, but I want you to grab ahold of some powerful words that someone told me that destroyed every lie the devil was telling me concerning my situation. Her exact words were, "Wherever there is life there is still hope." Hope is a powerful word. The definition of hope is there is still a chance, and some of the synonyms of hope are "faith, confidence, expectation and anticipation." What she was literally trying to tell me was since I was still alive, I still had a chance for God to change my entire situation around. During that time in my life I really didn't have much hope left, but Jesus loved me so much that He sent one of His servants to deposit some more hope in me. As I stated earlier, one of the definitions of hope is faith. God made sure that I received enough faith and hope to believe that He was capable and was going to change the situation I was in. I heard the Lord say, don't let your yesterday define who you are going to be tomorrow.

Due to how I was living and looking, no one ever would have thought that a great big righteous God would have had great big plans for a disobedient rebellious person like me. I can even remember during my addiction, my skin had such a dark ashy look that many of my friends were saying that it looked like death was on me. They had already counted me out, but Jesus had counted me in, so here I am over twenty-four years later, still alive with the ability to tell my story. I was in such bad shape that one day when I was in my addiction, a lady called herself ministering to me. She told me that the Lord told her to tell me that if I did not stop using drugs right then, He was not going to give me another opportunity to be saved. That was just the devil and a lie from the pit of hell. Don't ever let anyone count you out. Don't ever let anyone cause you to believe that the God who sent His Son to die for your sins would send a message to you like that. The Lord knows that we cannot stop doing anything without His help. Due to all the demonic spirits I was battling, if I had the power to stop using drugs on my own, I would had stopped a long time ago. I would have looked in the mirror one day and said that is it.

Many of us were born in sin and shapen in iniquity. According to the Strong's Concordance, the word *shapen* means "formed"; therefore, we were formed, shaped, designed and molded in iniquity. A lot of times we look at people and say, "I am not as messed up as they are." It was actually another drug addict who looked at me one day and told me I needed Jesus, as if she didn't. When we make comments like that to people, what we are actually saying is I am not formed, shaped, designed and molded as bad as you are. And that may be true, but I do not believe that people always choose to be in the shape that they end up in. It hurts my heart when I see people look down on people who have ended up in situations that they didn't necessarily have any control over.

I believe that Satan uses trickery, deception and manipulation to cause many people to end up in the shape that they are in. The Bible says he is more subtle than any beast of the field.

The devil will allow us to see the effect that drugs are having on another person and trick us by telling us that if we use the drugs, we will be strong enough not to allow the drugs to take us as far as it has taken everybody else. He lies to us and tells us that we will be strong enough to quit whenever we get ready too. At least that is the lie he told me. It is pride that would cause us to believe such a lie. Now I see why the Bible says that pride goes before destruction and a haughty spirit before a fall. Thinking that I would be strong enough to stop using drugs whenever I got ready to had literally torn my life apart during those years I was battling the addictions that had plagued my life. I often think about some of the evil things the devil did to me back then when I did not have the ability to know about many of his tricks. He had taken my integrity, my looks, and everything else I had, and I still had the nerve to still have some pride left.

How can you be beat down and broke and still have pride? The devil is a mess! We should all pray and ask God to show us the spirits of pride that are operating in our lives. There is hidden pride, little pride, big pride and sneaky pride. Pride lodges in the deepest crevices of our hearts. The Bible says that our hearts are deceitful and desperately wicked, who can know it (Jeremiah 17:9). I will tell you Who can know it, GOD. God knows all about us; He knows our weaknesses and our strengths. Life will be so much easier for us if we listen to God when He is trying to deal with us and bring correction to us in different areas of our lives. My constant prayer to God is, "Please help me not to be a rebellious daughter to You." When you have dealt with drugs, strong spirits of rebellion will try to lodge and operate in your life. If we are not prayerful, we will find ourselves protecting, pampering and making excuses for those spirits too. We have to fall out of agreement with every spirit that is not like God. This is the season that we need to walk worthy of the vocation in which we are called. The Bible says rebellion is as the sin of witchcraft. These spirits work against God, not with God. If you are already saved and you are reading this book, repeat after me and say, "Lord, please don't allow me to be a rebellious Christian." Drugs have destroyed so many people's lives. Many have even died in their addiction. Sin takes on all types of forms and shapes. The devil has formed some people into murderers, perverts, alcoholics, and some into drug addicts etc. Whatever the devil forms a person into, Jesus can transform them. That word *transform* means that Jesus will alter, change, renovate and convert you.

Although I was caught up and strung out on drugs, God did not allow the devil to kill me. I believe God left me here so that people can see His miracle-working power. Since God has allowed me to live through all that I have been through in my life, I must declare His works and not be ashamed to tell people about the many wonderful works that God has performed in my life. As I began to ponder about all those things, I came to the conclusion that there could have been various reasons that I had to go through some of the things that I had encountered. My first thought was, maybe God allowed those things so that I would have the ability to let somebody else know that wherever there is life, there is still hope and that there is a light at the end of the tunnel. You must understand that your (life) book doesn't have to end messed up, because Jesus is the Author and the Finisher of our faith (Hebrews 12:2). An author is a professional writer and a finisher is someone who gives something or somebody its final improvements and enhancements. Your life, (story or book) is so unique and it is not like anybody else's. Jesus, the Author, is professionally writing your book and He, the Finisher, is able to make those final improvements and enhancements in your life.

Although living my life as a drug addict was very hard and unpleasant, now I am grateful for the things that I have been through, because now I know firsthand how a person who is bound by drugs may be feeling and why they end up doing some of the things that they do. Now I have an understanding of how defenseless they are without Jesus. Pride will make us think that we can make it without Jesus. That is why the Bible lets us know that pride goes before destruction and a haughty spirit before a fall. Drugs have destroyed many people's lives. But God has also delivered many people from drugs. God wants to make you His trophy. He wants to deliver you and show you off to the world. The Bible says eyes haven't seen, ears haven't heard, neither has it entered into the heart of man what God has in store for you. But you will never be able to accomplish it without Jesus! Jesus is the Vine and we are the branches. A branch that is disconnected from its vine cannot grow and will eventually die. We cannot grow without Jesus. We cannot change for the better without Jesus. We cannot do anything without Jesus. Once we come to this conclusion, our lives will take a drastic change. The Bible says you shall know the truth and the truth shall set you free! And who the Son has set free is free in deed.

As you continue reading the pages of this book, it is my prayer that God will deposit a new level of faith on the inside of you that will launch you into your God-ordained destiny. I also pray that your spiritual understanding will be enlightened so that you will have the ability to overcome every obstacle, trap, trick and snare that our adversary the devil sends your way. That you would have the ability to make the right choices for your life this day forward as you are led by God's Spirit.

Although I hate to tell you this, I must let you know that just as God has a destiny for our lives, the devil has a destiny for our lives too. But we have the ability to choose if we want the destiny that God has ordained for our life or the one the devil has ordained for our life.

> *Deuteronomy 30:19*
> *I call heaven and earth to record this day against you, that I have set before you life and death, blessing and cursing: therefore choose life, that both thou and thy seed may live.*

Once you choose blessings, life and God's way, God will bless you with everything that you will need on your journey in order to fulfill your destiny that He has already mapped out for you. God may bless you with a mentor, or either He will just allow you to watch the lives of others from afar. As you grow in the Lord, He will one day raise you up to mentor someone or have others watching your life from afar.

Don't be discouraged by what you may be going through right now. Maybe you are going through a particular trial so that you will have the ability to walk somebody else through what they are going through. Who can be a better example to someone than someone who has already been down that same road and made it?

> *Hebrews 5:2*
> *Who can have compassion on the ignorant, and on them that are out of the way; for that he himself also is compassed with infirmity.*

> *Ezekiel 3:15*
> *Then I came to them of the captivity at Telabib,*

that dwelt by the river of Chebar, and I sat where
they sat, and remained there astonished among
them seven days.

According to the Scriptures, the captives of Judah were
deported to a place called Tel Abib in the land of Babylon.

Whenever you see Judah, Judah means "praise" and the
name Tel-abib means "mound of the deluge" because it was
flooded by the Euphrates River. It is not exactly clear where
the Biblical Tel-abib was located, but many scholars believe
it was near Nippur, about fifty miles southeast of Babylon.

The word *deluge* means "a flood or rainstorm." The devil
loves to flood our lives with other types of spirits that we
end up needing deliverance from, along with the spirit of
addiction. The enemy is able to flood our lives with all
different types of spirits, because once we get addicted to
the drugs, we are almost willing to do anything to get them.
Drugs will cause us to lie, cheat, steal, manipulate and
deceive people while our hearts are continually being
hardened and darkened so that we will carry evil wicked
deceitful plans out in order to get high. This may be the
condition you are in right now. You also may be in a
spiritual storm, but God is able to cause the storm to cease
in your life. I believe that a drug addiction is one of the
worst storms that anybody can encounter in his or her life.
I have been through it. Let's look at that in the natural.
People lose a lot of things sometimes from a storm—their
homes and some even their very lives. I had lost my
integrity, my hope, my looks, my apartment, my car and
even my job.

Also notice that Tel-abib was fifty miles from Babylon, and
Babylon means "a place of confusion." Confusion means

"mixed up, bewildered, or perplexed." When we are on drugs, our minds are so confused that we cannot make sound decisions. Some of us have also made some decisions that could have cost us our very life. The confused mental state that I was in, along with the spiritual storm that I encountered, blew me around so bad that I was living like a vagabond. A vagabond is a person who wanders from place to place. During a spiritual storm, winds can be so boisterous that you do not have any control over your life. I believe that when we are out there on drugs, our motto is: anyway the wind blows is cool with me as long as it blows me to a place where I can get more drugs. That is a very dangerous place to be. I have even jumped back in cars with men that I knew I had previously ripped off because I was so desperate for another hit off of the cocaine pipe. I was playing Russian roulette with my life because those men could have killed me. We all know that people do not play around with their money. I can also remember one night when I was out in the cold and the snow was up to my knees as I was trying to walk up a hill trying to get some more money to buy one more bag of cocaine.

The prophet Ezekiel was among the first to be taken captive to Babylon. According to the Bible, he lived at a place called Tel-abib, which was by the River Chebar or (grand canal).

The "river" has been identified as the "Naru Kabari" because of two cuneiform inscriptions from Nippur. According to these tablets, there was an irrigation canal that brought the water of the Euphrates River from Nippur to Babylon and looped around to the River near Erech. The canal's modern name is Shatt en-Nil.

The Jewish colonists were treated rather well, and the

prophet Jeremiah sent them a message from Jerusalem to take wives, build houses, plant gardens and take advantage of their situation because they were going to be there for seventy years.

The prophet Jeremiah was sent to tell the people to go on and get settled down in their present condition because they were going to be there for a while.

> *Jeremiah 29:28*
> *For therefore he sent unto us in Babylon, saying, This captivity is long: build ye houses, and dwell in them; and plant gardens, and eat the fruit of them.*

I would admonish you to read the whole twenty-ninth chapter of the book of Jeremiah. It lets us know that sometimes because of our rebellion and the decisions that we make in life, we can end up in that situation or state for a long time. Drugs is not a place that anyone should try to visit and feel like they are going to have the strength to say I am not going back to that place anymore. Drugs are a stronghold; it is a demon. A stronghold is a fortified place, a secure place. I would even like to say that it is like maximum security in a prison. But Jesus came to set the captives free. He is the only real antidote, cure, or remedy for any type of addiction. Keep this in mind. I was twelve years old when I smoked my first cigarette, took my first drink of alcohol, and smoked my first joint, then things began to accelerate after that. I was thirty-one years old when I finally got delivered from it all, and I pray that I will never play with any of it again in Jesus' name.

You do the math; nineteen years is a long time to be in captivity. And I give all the praises to God that I am still alive to be able to tell my story. I saw death so many times out there that I lost count of all the crazy situations I ended up in. I am so blessed to be alive, and I am not ashamed or embarrassed to share things in this book that others would probably not dare to share, because I am now a new creature in Christ. Old things have passed away, and all things have become new. That old person no longer lives, because the life I now live I live by faith in the Son of God. That means that it is no longer I that live, but Christ is living on the inside of me. When God delivers you from drugs, do not start perpetually backsliding. Run for your life. Live for God. I am not trying to scare you. But some people make it back and some don't. I know several people who backslid and died in a backslidden state. The Bible tells us that the righteous will scarcely make it in, so where will the ungodly and the sinner appear on that day when the Lord returns? The devil is working hard every day trying to cause people to backslide.

1 Peter 4:18
And if the righteous scarcely be saved, where shall the ungodly and the sinner appear?

Luke 11:24-26
When the unclean spirit is gone out of a man, he walketh through dry places, seeking rest; and finding none, he saith, I will return unto my house whence I came out.

And when he cometh, he findeth it swept and garnished.

Then goeth he and taketh to him seven other spirits more wicked than himself; and they enter in, and dwell there: and the last state of that man is worse than the first.

Matthew 24:13
But he that shall endure unto the end, the same
shall be saved.

Take heed to the scriptures that I am writing in this book. It would be wise to memorize them if you do not already know them. The Word of God is the most powerful weapon that we have. In Ephesians chapter 6, the Word of God is referred to as the Sword of the Spirit.

2 Corinthians 5:17
Therefore if any man be in Christ, he is a new
creature: old things are passed away; behold, all
things are become new.

Galatians 2:20
I am crucified with Christ: nevertheless I live;
yet not I, but Christ liveth in me: and the life
which I now live in the flesh I live by the faith of
the Son of God, who loved me, and gave himself
for me.

Jesus is greater, stronger, mightier, and more powerful than any demonic spirit. And whom the Son (Jesus) sets free is free indeed.

1 John 4:4
Ye are of God, little children, and have overcome
them: because greater is he that is in you, than
he that is in the world.

John 8:36 If the Son therefore shall make you
free, ye shall be free indeed.

Always remember you are no match for the devil, drugs, alcohol, gambling, fornication, or any of the devil's spirits without Jesus! But with Jesus, You Can Make It.

-*Five*-
THE POWER OF KNOWING OUR SPIRITUAL RIGHTS

Why did I really have to endure the pain, agony and embarrassment that I experienced living my life as a crack head and heroin addict? Was the main reason because of the sins of my father? After all, he did do a lot of rotten things. Or was the devil just taking advantage of me because I did not know my spiritual rights? I had no idea that Jesus had already paid the price for my sins and the sins of my father and his father and his father's father. . . I also didn't know we now have a better covenant! The devil takes advantage of people who do not know their spiritual rights. This is why when people are arrested for a crime in the natural, they usually hire a lawyer who is more familiar with the law and their rights than they are. Make sure you stay connected with other believers who are familiar with sound doctrine.

Hosea 4:6
My people are destroyed for lack of knowledge:
because thou hast rejected knowledge, I will also
reject thee, that thou shalt be no priest to me:

2 Timothy 4:3
For the time will come when they will not endure
sound doctrine; but after their own lusts shall

*they heap to themselves teachers, having itching
ears;*

Proverbs 1:5
*A wise man will hear, and will increase learning;
and a man of understanding shall attain unto
wise counsels:*

2 Timothy 2:15
*Study to shew thyself approved unto God, a
workman that needeth not to be ashamed, rightly
dividing the word of truth.*

Some people do not want to hear or receive sound doctrine
because they still want to hold on to the things of the world.
But if God delivers you from drugs, you better try to learn
sound doctrine, find out every weapon, benefit and gift that
you are entitled to because you are going to need them. Do
not be sending out mixed messages. You better let the devil
know that you are serving Jesus and Him only will you
serve!

Jesus has already paid the price for every sin that we have
committed. Let's just say we have a "get out of jail" free
card, but many people stay in jail because they don't know
they have already been bonded out. I can remember when I
was in school I read a story about these people who were in
captivity so long. When one of them got set free, he tried to
get the other ones to go with him, but they didn't want to
go. They had gotten so attached and familiar with their
captivity that they did not want to be free. But if you desire
to be free, Jesus will set you free.

THE POWER OF THE TONGUE

My next question is, was I constantly going through some of the things that I was going through because death and life are in the power of the tongue and Momma and Grandmother didn't know that every time they spoke negative words over my life, saying I was just like my daddy, I looked just like him, acted like him and I lied just like him, they were forming my life, but in a negative way. We have to pray and ask God to tame our tongue because the Bible lets us know that we can't tame it ourselves. That word *tame* means "to train or discipline." It may take some time, but the Lord will discipline our tongue if we really want Him to. I really had a problem in that area and the Lord has helped me tremendously. My mouth was like a garbage can. Every other word was a curse word before I got saved, but God gave me a miracle. However, every now and then the devil still tries to put thoughts in my mind of things to say to get someone told.

Living saved is a constant battle, but the Lord can and will deliver us from every evil work. The tongue is such a powerful force, and now I know I can speak, plant and sow positive words into my own life and the lives of others. I can prophesy blessings over my own life and the lives of others. I can also bind and pluck up from the root every negative word that has been spoken over my life and the lives of others. Right now in the name of Jesus I pluck up from the root every negative word that has been spoken over our lives. Don't hang around people who always have something negative to say about you. You need to be around people who can edify you, build you up and see good things for your life. It is my prayer that God will surround you with anointed people; strong apostles and prophets who can speak positive things into your life that will build you up, stir you up and comfort you. I also decree that your discernment will be keen and that you will have the ability to see when someone means you more harm than good. I decree you will have the strength to separate yourself from those who desire your hurt. I decree that you will have the ability to have and maintain a pure heart, in Jesus' name.

~Seven~

THE SPIRIT OF
REJECTION

My father abused my mother and every time she looked at me, she saw him because, of course, I did look just like him. That has to be a hard pill to swallow, to have to raise a child who looks exactly like somebody who has probably caused you to be filled with a lot of hurt and rejection yourself. Due to the way my father treated my mother, I didn't have the pleasure of being raised by my mother and father. My mother and grandmother raised me. Children need their fathers. I was told that Daddy didn't want me anyway; he tried to give Momma some toothache medicine to cause her to self-abort me. Maybe since I was rejected from the womb, his rejection caused me to go out into the world and try to find love in all the wrong places. Some people who suffer from rejection try to find circles where they are accepted. They do not know that we are already accepted in the Beloved. Rejection is the sense of being unwanted, the agony of desperately wanting people to love you but being convinced that they don't.

Maybe your mother, your father, your spouse, or even some friends have rejected you. If so, God is going to show you as you continue to turn the pages of this book how much He loves you, because God is going to heal you and deliver you from that crippling spirit of rejection. Sometimes, a person can actually love, honor respect and accept you, but when you are suffering from rejection, you are unable to believe it or receive it. It is a hurting feeling to desire to be a part of something, but deep inside you don't feel that you are. Some people who suffer from rejection are usually always suspicious and they find it very hard to trust people. Many rejected people are willing to be used or mistreated, just to be accepted by people or be a part of something.

However, if the person who is suffering from rejection has a lot of leadership ability on the inside of them, in most cases, they will usually go to any height to make a name for themselves. And once a person is determined to make a name for themselves, there is nobody who can stop them but God. When a person tries to make a name for themselves, this also causes a spirit of confusion to come into their life.

> *Genesis 11:4-9*
> *And they said, Go to, let us build us a city and a tower, whose top may reach unto heaven; and let us make us a name, lest we be scattered abroad upon the face of the whole earth.*
>
> *And the Lord came down to see the city and the tower, which the children of men builded.*
>
> *And the Lord said, Behold, the people is one, and they have all one language; and this they begin to do: and now nothing will be restrained from them, which they have imagined to do.*
>
> *Go to, let us go down, and there confound their language, that they may not understand one another's speech.*

So the Lord scattered them abroad from thence upon the face of all the earth: and they left off to build the city.

Therefore is the name of it called Babel; because the Lord did there confound the language of all the earth: and from thence did the Lord scatter them abroad upon the face of all the earth.

I really made a big name for myself out there. I had a reputation out of this world. Everything I learned how to do I became real good at it, from shoplifting to picking pockets. Even in sin I was a natural-born leader, not a follower. Now God has made me a spiritual leader. The devil meant the things that he did to me for evil, but God brought good out of it. God is divinely strategic. He allowed a lot of people to know me in St. Louis, Missouri, where I was raised for twenty of the first twenty-two years of my life. Then He allowed me to move up here to Chicago, where I was well known in the different arenas I found myself in. Now I have the ability to go back to let all of my old associates see the before and the after. They knew me when I was a sinner and now they get to see me as a Christian. Many of them can tell my testimony much better than I can. God truly gave me a miracle when He saved me.

Joseph's brothers rejected him because they felt rejected by their father. They thought that their father loved Joseph more than he loved them, so they decided to get rid of Joseph, but because God was with him, He allowed everything that he went through to be a part of his making. Joseph's brothers needed to be accepted by him in the end to the extent they even lied and told him that their father had left specific instructions for Joseph before he died for Joseph to forgive his brothers for the things they had done to him. Joseph's brothers knew that whatever a man sows he shall also reap, but because God had delivered Joseph from the rejection, hurt and pain that his brothers had caused him, Joseph was able to love and treat his brothers as if they had never caused him any harm at all. Joseph knew that if he had not gone through the process that he had went through, he never would have ended up with the character and attributes that he needed in order to become the governor over the whole land of Egypt. We all need to know that when we all come to God, we are a work in progress and we need to allow Him to make us the person He designed for us to be.

THE SPIRIT OF
ADDICTION

According to Wikipedia, the free on-line encyclopedia, an addiction is "the continued repetition of a behavior despite adverse or unfavorable consequences." My personal definition of an addiction is a habit; a weakness and continuous ungodly cycle that causes people to do things they thought they would never do, including jeopardizing their lives and the lives of others in order to get the gratification they need by feeding their addiction. For example, the continued use of drugs in spite of health problems that can occur, or even death.

There are a variety of bad addictions that people struggle with. Some people struggle with drug addictions, alcohol addictions, gambling addictions, sex addictions, eating addictions, shopping addictions and many other types of addictions. Nobody knows better than you what addiction(s) you may be struggling with at the moment. Due to the fact an addiction is nothing to be proud of, we have what are called closet addicts. A closet addict is a person who tries very hard to hide their addiction(s). One way to really figure out what your addiction(s) are is by asking yourself what it is that you spend the majority of your money on, what you spend the majority of your time doing and/or what it is that you need in order to function properly. Every addiction has its own attributes and consequences.

Every bad addiction is a demonic spirit and the spirit of addiction is the ruling spirit. A ruling spirit is a spirit that is in charge of telling the lower-ranking spirits in their class what to do. For example, the spirit of addiction is the ruling spirit and some of the lower-ranking spirits under its command are: spirits of cocaine, spirits of heroine, spirits of marijuana, spirits of gambling, a spirit of gluttony, a spirit of nicotine, a spirit of lust, etc. With this in mind, after you have dealt with the lower-ranking spirits that have held you in captivity, you must also get rid of the ruling spirit. If you allow the ruling spirit to remain in your life, it will have the ability to cause you to take on other forms of addictions.

Some people who stop getting high off of street drugs, such as cocaine, tend to end up with a coffee addiction, the spirit of caffeine. They cannot function without a cup of coffee, because coffee has now become their new addiction, because they did not deal with the ruling spirit of addiction. I believe the devil even causes the smell of coffee to be an addiction to some people. They just love to smell that fresh coffee brewing. Caffeine is defined as a drug. According to Wikipedia, caffeine is a bitter, white crystalline xanthine alkaloid and a stimulant drug. Caffeine and cocaine are both stimulant drugs, but cocaine is more harmful and more addictive than coffee.

An example of keeping ruling spirits alive is found in I Samuel 15:1-3 and I Samuel 15:18–21. In this particular passage of Scripture, Samuel, who was an anointed prophet of the Lord, sent King Saul (the anointed and appointed king over the children of Israel, God's chosen people) to get rid of the Amalekites. He was told to utterly destroy *all that they had and to spare them not.* He specifically told him to slay man and woman, infant and suckling, ox and shew camel and ass. In I Samuel 15:20, we see that Saul destroyed all of the Amalekites, but he left Agag, the king of the Amalekites, alive. The king is always the ruling spirit. Saul did not follow the instructions of the Lord; he kept the ruling spirit alive.

In I Samuel 15:21, Saul also allowed the people to take of the spoil, sheep and oxen—the chief of the things—that should have been utterly destroyed. And their excuse was they wanted to sacrifice those things to the Lord. The spoil, sheep, oxen and the chief things represent money or material things. Some people have a money addiction, meaning they end up willing to do anything for money, such as work a lot of overtime on their jobs, lie, cheat, steal gamble, sell their bodies, mess up their health and even risk their lives for it. **Whatever type of addiction a person may have, it usually takes money to buy it.** People with money addictions are very greedy and usually hoarders. Hoarders are people who accumulate things and refuse to give anything away. They are misers, ungenerous, stingy, selfish people. When a person loves money, they are also usually very rebellious. The Bible says:

> *1 Timothy 6:10*
> *For the love of money is the root of all evil: which while some coveted after, they have erred from the faith, and pierced themselves through with many sorrows.*

Roots help a plant to absorb water and nutrients from the soil. They anchor a plant firmly and also store food. It is the water and nutrients from the soil that cause plants to grow, so when we love money it causes all types of evil spirits to grow and be anchored on the inside of us. To be anchored means "to keep in place." Spirits of addiction are very stubborn spirits. They use all types of tactics in order to keep their domain in our lives. Demons refuse to move and that is why they have to be cast (thrown) out of our lives.

The second phrase from the Scripture says that while some covet after money, it causes them to err from the faith. To covet means "to want, crave, desire, or yearn to have." Matthew 6:24 lets us know that no man can serve two masters: for either he will hate the one, and love the other; or else he will hold to the one, and despise the other. We cannot serve God and mammon. Mammon is money. Every spirit has a voice, and we will always obey whatever or whoever we love the most. Many people have been known to leave the Lord because they loved money more than they loved the Lord.

It is usually always fulfilling to have something we want, or do something for someone we love. This is why in John 14:5, Jesus tells us, if we love Him, keep His commandments. Loving and building a relationship with Jesus is the key to breaking bad habits and forming good ones. The stronger our love for the Lord begins to develop, the more willing we are to let go of things that we know aren't pleasing to Him.

The problem with many of us who end up with addictions that are bad for us is that as people, especially if we are carnal, we tend to like, love, or lust after things, food and people who are not good for us. The devil only tempts us with things that we like or that he feels are irresistible to us.

James 1:13-15
Let no man say when he is tempted, I am tempted
of God: for God cannot be tempted with evil,

neither tempteth he any man: But every man is
tempted, when he is drawn away of his own lust,
and enticed. Then when lust hath conceived, it
bringeth forth sin: and sin, when it is finished,
bringeth forth death.

This scripture is the perfect picture of the way the spirit of addiction operates. To tempt means "to incite or stir up the desire on the inside of somebody." Once a person tries something and they begin to like it, the tempter comes regularly to stir up the desire for it until it becomes an addiction. At this stage, lust has conceived or caused that person to get pregnant and birth or bring forth the spirit of addiction; and if the addiction has the ability to take its full course that it desires to take, it will eventually bring forth death. This is why some people end up dying physically or spiritually. Those that die physically usually die of an overdose, car accident or getting killed from doing something wrong in order to feed the addiction they are battling. Regardless of the odds that are working against people that end up with an addiction, many people still get set free by the power of God.

As we look back at I Timothy 6:10, it tells us that the spirit of mammon will cause us to err from the faith. That word *err* means "to make a mistake or behave badly." Faith is what we believe, so when we err from the faith, we no longer obey the Scriptures and principles of God. We no longer have morals or a conviction when we treat people wrong or do wrong things. Our standards are lowered. If we begin to love money or get addicted to it, it gets harder and harder for us to obey the Scriptures. When this happens, this hinders us from being able to walk in the true blessings of the Lord. The Bible tells us:

Luke 6:38
Give, and it shall be given unto you; good measure, pressed down, and shaken together, and running over, shall men give into your bosom. For with the same measure that ye mete withal it shall be measured to you again.

Malachi 3:10
Bring ye all the tithes into the storehouse, that there may be meat in mine house, and prove me now herewith, saith the Lord of hosts, if I will not open you the windows of heaven, and pour you out a blessing, that there shall not be room enough to receive it.

These verses mean that if we believe and obey the Word of God, we will receive significantly much more than what we have given. If we pay our tithe, God can pour us out just one blessing that will be so big that we will not have enough room to receive the blessing. The blessings of Abraham will be so great in our lives, and we will be so blessed that we can be a blessing to others. God spoke to me one day and told me the reason that a lot of His people live in poverty is because they are too selfish and stingy to bless anybody else; and due to that behavior, God only has to bless them with enough to take care of themselves. God allows people who are willing to give and be a blessing to others to be His stewards. A steward is one who is chosen to manage the Lord's property and finances. Therefore, a steward is blessed and trusted with enough money and resources to bless others.

The spirit of mammon says hold on tight to everything you have. It trains people to be stingy, selfish, wicked hoarders. This spirit will allow people to watch other people be hungry and in need and not try to do anything to help them. In Luke 12, we see how this spirit operates and the consequences we suffer for allowing it to dominate our lives. It causes us to pierce ourselves with many sorrows just like I Timothy 6:10 says we would.

> *Luke 12:15-21 Amplified Bible (AMP)*
> *And He said to them, Guard yourselves and keep free from all covetousness (the immoderate desire for wealth, the greedy longing to have more); for a man's life does not consist in and is not derived from possessing [a] overflowing abundance or that which is [b] over and above his needs.*
>
> *Then He told them a parable, saying, The land of a rich man was fertile and yielded plentifully.*
>
> *And he considered and debated within himself, What shall I do? I have no place [in which] to gather together my harvest.*
>
> *And he said, I will do this: I will pull down my storehouses and build larger ones, and there I will store all [c] my grain or produce and my goods.*
>
> *And I will say to my soul, Soul, you have many good things laid up, [enough] for many years. Take your ease; eat, drink, and enjoy yourself merrily.*
>
> *But God said to him, You fool! This very night [d] they [the messengers of God] will demand your soul of you; and all the things that you have*

prepared, whose will they be?

So it is with the one who continues to lay up and
hoard possessions for himself and is not rich [in
his relation] to God [this is how he fares].

After the rich man built larger storehouses to store his
goods, he died and was unable to enjoy any of it. We have
to pay close attention to our ways. The devil is so subtle that
he will either have us in denial of our behavior, or he will
make us justify our wrong actions, attitudes and dispositions.
It is time for us to let go of all of the excuses that we have
come up with to hold on to things that the Lord has told us
to utterly destroy. For some of us, it is very easy to get
addicted to just about anything. This includes people,
places, or things; therefore, we must be careful with what
we touch, try, entertain, or get involved with in life. If we
refuse to get rid of the people and things that the Lord has
instructed us to utterly destroy or get rid of, those people or
things usually end up turning on us and will eventually try
to destroy us. It is because of the Lord's mercy we are not
consumed. Although we would hate to admit it, I believe
that the majority of us have often played Russian roulette
with our lives and/or salvation through being rebellious and
disobedient.

We must smite our enemies (demons) until they are utterly
destroyed. Demons will plead with us and beg us to let them
remain in our lives. We cannot make any covenants or
agreements with them. Demons are liars and you cannot
believe anything they say. They will lie to you and tell you
that they will benefit you if you allow them to stay around.
For instance, I had a fighting demon that would always try
to negotiate with me and tell me that if I got rid of him,
people would try to take advantage of me and run over me.

Demons are very crafty and subtle. The lie they told me worked for many, many years, even while I was saved. Finally, with the help of the Holy Spirit, I fell out of agreement with that fighting demon and refused to allow that demon to remain on the inside of me. I knew the Lord did not want me to fight in the natural because He created me to be a spiritual warrior. Demons will also promise us that they will control themselves if we let them stay. They promise they will not hurt us, but they are lying. For example, they will tell you to just smoke one bag of cocaine and you will have the ability to stop and go take care of the rest of your business, such as paying your rent and buying groceries for the house. You believe them and end up bound, hungry and broke again. We cannot afford to show demons any mercy because they are not going to show us any mercy.

There are some things that you are going to hear me saying over and over and over again, until you get it. The reason is if you have ever had a real battle with a spirit of addiction of any kind, you cannot afford to let these spirits back in your life. I used to minister at a shelter for women when I first got saved and I would tell them to remember the shape they were in before they came to the Lord and imagine themselves seven times worse. We all knew, including me, that if the devil had the opportunity to make us seven times worse, a lot of us might not have been able to survive any longer. Especially me, because I was out there real bad. This scripture, Luke 11:24-26, is the scripture that has helped me not to jump in and out of God. This scripture put a good type of fear in my heart, because it helped me not to play around with drug demons after I was finally set free.

The Lord told me that He is going to use me to be your spiritual Drill Sergeant as you continue to read this book.

I AM A DRILL SERGEANT

By the anointing of the Holy Spirit, I will assist each individual in their efforts to become a highly motivated, well disciplined, physically and mentally fit Spiritual Soldier, capable of defeating any enemy on this spiritual battlefield. The Holy Spirit, through me, will instill integrity and confidence, in everyone that the Holy Spirit uses me to train. They will have confidence in the Lord, confidence in self, confidence in the Army of the Lord and confidence in the Kingdom of God.

I will insist that each Soldier meet and maintain the Lord's standards of military bearing and courtesy, consistent with the Kingdom of God.

I will lead by example, never requiring a Soldier to attempt any task I would not do myself.

But first, last and always, I am a Spiritual Soldier, dedicated to defend the fundamental principles, values, ethics and beliefs, of the Kingdom of God against all spiritual enemies.

I am a Drill Sergeant.
It is very important that we get a strong foundation laid in our lives in order to stand against the wiles of the devil, and that we continue to learn how to fight with the help of the Holy Spirit. These scriptures will allow us to measure our lives and be able to determine whether we have

a strong foundation or a weak one. It is very important for us to know what condition our foundation is in at all times, so that we can make some corrective actions if needed.

•

Matthew 7:24-27
Therefore whosoever heareth these sayings of mine, and doeth them, I will liken him unto a wise man, which built his house upon a rock:

And the rain descended, and the floods came, and the winds blew, and beat upon that house; and it fell not: for it was founded upon a rock.

And every one that heareth these sayings of mine, and doeth them not, shall be likened unto a foolish man, which built his house upon the sand:

And the rain descended, and the floods came, and the winds blew, and beat upon that house; and it fell: and great was the fall of it.

This passage of scripture allows us to know that if we walk in obedience and do the things the Lord tell us to do, we will be strong and will not have to worry about falling, backsliding, or becoming a casualty. It also tells us that if we are disobedient, we will be constantly falling and backsliding, which can cause us to end up being a casualty. We have to learn how to fight in the Spirit because this is not a natural fight. It is a spiritual one! If this were a natural fight, many of us would have won the battle a long time ago, because many of us were natural-born fighters. Well, now it is time for us to learn how to roll up our spiritual sleeves and fight, because we might not have to fight to get free, but we are definitely going to have to fight to stay free.

Ephesians 6:12
For we wrestle not against flesh and blood, but against principalities, against powers, against the rulers of the darkness of this world, against spiritual wickedness in high places.

Because this is not a natural battle and it is a spiritual one, we cannot see our enemy with our natural eyes. We must be born of the Spirit so that our spiritual eyes, ears and nose can be open to the things of God.

John 3:5–7
Jesus answered, Verily, verily, I say unto thee, Except a man be born of water and of the Spirit, he cannot enter into the kingdom of God.

That which is born of the flesh is flesh; and that which is born of the Spirit is spirit.

Marvel not that I said unto thee, Ye must be born again.

Ephesians 1:17–22
That the God of our Lord Jesus Christ, the Father of glory, may give unto you the spirit of wisdom and revelation in the knowledge of him:

The eyes of your understanding being enlightened; that ye may know what is the hope of his calling, and what the riches of the glory of his inheritance in the saints,

*And what is the exceeding greatness of his power
to us-ward who believe, according to the working
of his mighty power,*

*Which he wrought in Christ, when he raised him
from the dead, and set him at his own right hand
in the heavenly places,*

*Far above all principality, and power, and might,
and dominion, and every name that is named, not
only in this world, but also in that which is to
come:*

*And hath put all things under his feet, and gave
him to be the head over all things to the church.*

Ephesians 3:16
*That he would grant you, according to the riches
of his glory, to be strengthened with might by his
Spirit in the inner man;*

Our inner man is our spiritual man. Once we are born of the Spirit, our spiritual man comes alive. Remember the scripture in John 3:6 that says that which is born of the flesh is flesh and that which is born of the Spirit is spirit. If you are not saved, born again, this is a good time for you to ask the Lord to come into your life and give you a born-again experience, because you will never be able to defeat the enemy with any of your fleshly abilities. This is why we must learn spiritual warfare.

Our mind is the battleground. The enemy tries to plant thoughts in our minds to tempt us to do the wrong thing so that he can enter back on the inside of us. We always have a better advantage fighting the enemy when he is living on the outside of us than when he is operating on the inside. This is why the Bible tells us to cast down every imagination and every high thing that exalts itself against the knowledge of God. Demons will begin to tell us things, such as, "Aren't you bored? Don't you miss me? Well, come on and let's go get high and have fun like we used to." They will begin to make us remember the good times, but they will never remind us of the pain they caused us in our addiction. At times we can find ourselves having selective amnesia. Therefore, I always ask the Holy Spirit to bring all things back to my remembrance and remind me of the pain drugs have caused me when the devil starts talking to me. This gives me the strength and ability to cast those old drug memories of the past down. Although we were battling an addiction, I am sure we all had good days and bad days. However, the end result was far worse than the beginning. At least for me it was. I don't ever want to look like I was looking in the latter days of my addiction, and I certainly don't want to live that horrible lifestyle again. That turned out to be some hard living. Don't entertain the devil; instead, cast those thoughts down. This will take a lot of discipline, because you have to bring your thoughts into captivity so that you can obey the Lord.

2 Corinthians 10:5
Casting down imaginations, and every high thing that exalteth itself against the knowledge of God, and bringing into captivity every thought to the obedience of Christ;

Sometimes, no matter how hard you try to cast those imaginations down, it may appear that the devil will begin to talk more and louder. This is another reason why you have to learn spiritual warfare. The more battles you fight and the more battles you win, the more spiritually strong, experienced, and skillful you will become. The Word of the Lord tells us that we have the keys to the kingdom, and whatever we bind on earth will be bound in heaven. You have to bind up the voice of the enemy, so tell him to shut up in Jesus' name!

> *Matthew 16:19*
> *And I will give unto thee the keys of the kingdom of heaven: and whatsoever thou shalt bind on earth shall be bound in heaven: and whatsoever thou shalt loose on earth shall be loosed in heaven.*

Keys represent authority. Know that as you begin to bind the voice of the enemy on earth God is going to bind him in heaven. To bind means "to tie up, stop, lock, or put an end to." To loose means "to unlock, release, set free, or let go." You have to utilize the authority that has been given to you. The Bible also tells us that if we submit ourselves to God and resist the devil, he will flee from us. To resist means "to fight, attack, struggle, counterattack, oppose, defy, contest, or challenge."

> *James 4:7*
> *Submit yourselves therefore to God. Resist the devil, and he will flee from you.*

Every person's level of warfare is different, and I believe that our level of warfare depends on five things.

1. How valuable we were to the kingdom of darkness.
Many of us were very valuable to the kingdom of darkness, because whatever Satan told us to do, we not only did it, but we were experts at carrying out the assignments that he sent us on. Many of us caused a lot of people to suffer because

of our addiction, and the devil loves to see people suffer. The demons that were in us used to use us to steal from people, depress them, aggravate them, frustrate them, and cause our loved ones to worry about us all the time. Notice that when people go on a job interview, the employer will most likely hire the one with the most experience. They will even pay them according to the amount of experience that person has. No employer wants to take out the time to train somebody without experience to do a job if they don't have to. Well, Satan had trained many of us how to carry out his will really good in some of the ways I mentioned earlier. But he also trained many of us on how to get other people addicted to whatever we were addicted to, and we had probably been addicted a long time. That means we were not only experienced at what we were doing, but we also had enough time to help mess up a lot of other people's lives.

This is why in Luke 11:24, when the devil is cast out of a person, he says that he is going to go back into his house that he came out of because that person is already experienced, and he (Satan) is very pleased with the way they were doing things. Satan is so angry about losing that person that the Bible says once the unclean spirit is cast out it brings seven more spirits with him more wicked than himself because he is determined to get back in. The devil is so furious and mad that he lost many of us that he will always continue to fight us. This is why it is mandatory that we learn how to fight with the spiritual weapons God has given us. We must learn how to fast and pray in order to keep the demons out of our lives. The devil is so confident that he is going to get back on the inside of us that one of his statements is that he is going to go back into the very house that he just came out of. This is a very possessive statement. It is up to us to allow the devil to know that our body is no longer his house. Our body is now the temple of the Holy Ghost. He will never understand that our body is not his house anymore if we allow him to keep running in and out of our bodies at will. Some of us need to put a sign that says SOLD in the front of our spiritual house, and when the devil comes to knock on the door, make sure that we allow the Holy Ghost and not our flesh to answer the door.

2. How big of a threat we are to the kingdom of darkness. The more you love the Lord, the bigger the threat you are to the kingdom of darkness. Luke 7:47 tells us that whoever is forgiven much loves much. When the Lord has delivered a person from an addiction that has really had them messed up badly, that person usually loves the Lord a whole lot and is very grateful. The Bible says that if we love the Lord, we will keep His commandments; meaning that fulfilling the devil's assignments begin to decrease and fulfilling the Lord's assignments begin to increase. Also, if we are humble, that really makes it hard on the kingdom of darkness because Satan knows that if we humble ourselves, we will be exalted in due time. To exalt means "to promote or raise up." The enemy can't stand to see us grow in the Lord. Remember, his main objective is to kill, steal, and destroy. As we begin to grow in the Lord, we have the ability to teach, train, lay strong foundations in others, heal, deliver, and set other people free in Jesus' name. The student grows up and becomes the teacher. The more valuable we become to the kingdom of God, the greater threat we become to the kingdom of darkness. Now we are tearing down the things that we once built. We are tearing the devil's kingdom down.

Always remember, the more people we get to enlist in the army of the Lord, this causes the enemy's army to get smaller and weaker. Don't ever think we are going to be able to just tear the devil's kingdom down without him trying to fight us back. The Lord recently sent me to preach at a church, and He had me minister about no matter how many times the children of Israel whipped the Syrians, the Syrians were always trying to figure out how they would be able to whip the children of Israel. The Syrians were relentless. They never gave up. This is how we are going to have to be. RELENTLESS. No matter what the devil throws at us, we are going to have to be relentless and never give up. Press in and fulfill the destiny that the Lord has assigned for your life. Always remember that if God is for us, He is more than the whole world against us. And God has given us power over all the power of the enemy, and nothing shall by any means hurt us. The devil knows that we are a big threat to his kingdom, so it is very important for us to know who we are and how big of a threat we are to the kingdom of darkness. Greater is He, JESUS, that is in us than he that is in the world.

3. How many people will get saved, healed, and delivered through our ministry. One thing the devil hates most is to see new souls coming into the kingdom of God. This means that every time someone decides they are going to get saved that is one less person that Satan has in his army. God is very strategic. He knows how to set you up real good so that many people will get saved through your ministry. You would be surprised at how many people have gotten saved just by watching your life, and you didn't even know they got saved because of your stand in God, or because they saw the before and after picture of your life. When people really get excited about what the Lord has done for them, they have to run and tell somebody else. The Bible tells us that when Jesus got through witnessing to the woman at the well and told her everything she had ever done, she ran into the town and evangelized the whole town. Her words were,

"Come and see a Man who told me everything I have ever done." Jesus's prophetic gift got her attention. The Bible also talks about when Jesus began to heal people that His fame went throughout the earth, and many people began to follow Him. It is important for us to cast out devils, lay hands on the sick so that they can recover, prophesy, and come behind in no great gift. When people begin to see the power of God manifesting in our lives, they will begin to ask the question, "What must I do to be saved?" One day I was in a store in Roseland after the Lord had saved me and cast all of those demons out of me. I ran into a young lady that knew how strung out on drugs I was. I never got a chance to open my mouth to tell her what the Lord had done for me. Her immediate response was, "Jackie, I know that if the Lord helped you, He can help me." The reason she said that was because I was one of the worse ones out there, and I looked worse than any of the other drug addicts that we were in association with. She knew it was not a rehab that had helped me; she even knew it had to be the Lord. The Bible tells us to be walking epistles read of men. An epistle is a letter. She, a sinner, was able to look at my life and read my story. The way we live our lives is the greatest message we will ever preach.

4. How great our destiny is. Our destiny is our purpose; the reason we were born. Jesus said for this very reason He had come to the earth was to destroy the works of the devil. Many of you have great destinies that are going to be fulfilled, because God is not a man that He should lie, neither is He the Son of Man that He should repent. If He spoke it He shall surely bring it to pass. Yes, it's coming to pass. Your very destiny has the devil frustrated, and he is trying to figure out a way he can keep your destiny from being fulfilled. My advice to you is to not allow anybody or anything to deter you from your purpose. The enemy sometimes brings people in our lives to try to hinder us from fulfilling our destiny. The Scripture says in Galatians 3:1, "Who has bewitched you that you could not obey the truth," and Galatians 5:7 says, "Ye did run well; who did hinder you that you should not obey the truth?" When God tells you to separate from people who are walking in carnality and trying to get you to compromise, be obedient and separate. That word *bewitched* means "to cast a spell on somebody." This would be a relationship that you know the person doesn't mean you any good, but you just can't seem to shake them loose. When you are caught up in something like that, my advice to you would be to fast and pray. For those that do not know, fasting means "to refrain from eating as the Lord leads you."

How much the Lord will allow you to fast will depend on your health. Do not get so desperate that you hurt yourself from fasting too much. Satan has a lot of tricks up his sleeve to try to stop us. The Bible tells us to be wise as serpents and harmless as doves. The devil cannot outsmart you as long as you allow God to equip you for the destiny that He has called you to walk in. I can hear the Lord saying, "Eyes haven't seen, ears haven't heard the things that the Lord has in store for you." God did not allow you to still be alive and reading this book for nothing. He has a great destiny for you. Walk in it. Let your main goal be to hear the Father say, "This is my son or daughter in whom I am well pleased."

5. How bad our new lifestyle brings embarrassment to the kingdom of darkness. The devil hates to be embarrassed; Jesus already made a spectacle of him openly, which means He embarrassed him in front of a whole lot of people. When the devil has really had you trapped in a place of shame and embarrassment, and God begins to use your life to embarrass the devil back, the devil gets very angry and vindictive. As

I was going through a heavy period of warfare in my life, I asked the Lord why my warfare was so intense. Why is the enemy fighting me so hard? The Lord's answer to me was, "The devil is embarrassed because of everything that you have allowed Me to do in your life." I was a hardcore dope fiend before the Lord saved me, with no sense of direction. I had to borrow my first dress to go to church in. I now have two homeless shelters and a ministry where I preach to ex-addicts like I once was. Now I have thirteen paid employees on the payroll, and my name is signed on every one of their checks. God promised that He would make us the head and not the tail and that we would lend and not have to borrow.

God said, "When I saved you, if you would have just been a bench member and not allowed me to make you an entrepreneur and a preacher, your warfare would not be this great. The devil is mad because he had you homeless with a heroin and cocaine habit so bad that you could barely walk or comb your hair until you had gotten your next fix. He tried to kill you so many times that you lost count yourself, but I would not allow him to kill you." It is very embarrassing to the kingdom of darkness when the Lord saves a person and carries them from glory to glory. The devil doesn't mind us being saved as long as we are stuck or still carnal. We must understand that it is the will of the Lord Jesus, for each and every one of us, to prosper and be in health as our soul prospers. When God transforms our lives, the devil gets so embarrassed that he wants to get rid of the evidence.

3 John 1:2
Beloved, I wish above all things that thou mayest prosper and be in health, even as thy soul prospereth.

-Nine-

SPIRITUAL WEAPONS

As I was lying down trying to get some rest from a long day of work at my office, the Lord began to talk to me concerning what He wanted me to write in this portion of this book. I had already completed about eighty pages, and I thought that the time for publishing this book was soon approaching. It is funny how you could think you are writing the beginning of your book, but you are actually writing the middle or the end of it.

The Holy Spirit took me to this passage of Scripture (Romans 8:26–39) that we will be dealing with along with other verses, because it is very essential for you to know that the Holy Spirit wants to help us, if we will accept His help. As an ex-addict myself, I know how it feels to really want help from a drug addiction, or any other type of addiction, and not really know how to go about getting the help we really need. For instance, who can really help us or is there really any help out there for us? Because many of us have been brainwashed to believe once a dope fiend always a dope fiend, or that we will never get over whatever addiction that is plaguing our lives. This is so far from the truth, because with God nothing shall be impossible (Luke 1:37). There is no sickness He cannot heal. There is no addiction He cannot break. And there is no person that He cannot change. I don't know where you are in your spiritual life, or whether you are saved at all, but if you do not know the Holy Spirit, you need to learn who He is, get filled with the Holy Spirit, and learn everything there is to learn about Him. The Holy Spirit is a person, not a thing, and He has many attributes, qualities, and characteristics.

In John 14:16-17, Jesus is telling His disciples that He was going to pray to the Father (God), and He (God) shall give us another comforter that *He* may abide with us forever. Verse 17 says, "Even the Spirit of truth; whom the world cannot receive, because it seeth *Him* not, neither knoweth *Him:* But ye know *Him* for *He* dwelleth with you and shall be in you. First, I want you to notice how many times we see the word *He* and *Him,* so that you will know that the Holy Spirit is a person. We build relationships and friendships with people by communicating with them and spending time with them, don't we? Well, we need to communicate with the Holy Spirit so that we can develop a strong relationship and friendship with Him.

If you are battling with any type of addiction, I am almost positive that you have been in association with a lot of people who did not mean you any good, which has caused you to feel as though you just can't trust anybody. Well, let your guard down. You can trust the Holy Spirit because He will not hurt you. He is only here to help you. He has the help that we need that we cannot afford to turn down. He can help us so much that one of the devil's main tactics is to try to cause us to be afraid of the Holy Spirit. Don't be afraid of the Holy Spirit, because that will only cause you to shut Him out of your life. He has been protecting you and assisting you all this time without you even knowing it, so to shut Him out now will only hinder you from walking in the fullness of your destiny that God has already orchestrated for you to walk in. God has great plans for your life, and it is the Holy Spirit's job to make sure that you are able to tap into the treasures and the greatness that is already on the inside of you. The devil has covered those treasures and greatness on the inside of you with dirt. Maybe the dirt the devil is using to cover up your greatness and treasures is the spirit of addiction. The devil is known as the "covering cherub." There are some things that he will cover up or try to hide from you with hopes that you will never find out about, or tap into your greatness and treasures. The devil is terrified of you getting acquainted and filled with the Holy Spirit because he knows that you will never find out who you are or the greatness and the treasures that are on the inside of you without the assistance of the Holy Spirit, your helper. The Bible tells us that the Holy Ghost will lead and guide us into all truth.

2 Corinthians 4:7
But we have this treasure in earthen vessels, that the excellency of the power may be of God, and not of us.

As we gaze back upon John 14:16–17, during this time, Jesus was being elevated to go and sit on the right hand of the Father, so He left us the Holy Spirit, whom He called another Comforter. Being a comforter is one of the attributes that the Holy Spirit has that I spoke about earlier, when I said He has many qualities, attributes, and characteristics. A comforter is one who goes out of His way by doing any and everything that it is going to take in order to make sure we are comfortable. If you have an addiction, I know firsthand that you are probably in an uncomfortable situation. Your living situation is probably uncomfortable. Your financial situation is probably uncomfortable, and you are probably feeling uncomfortable about everything that appears to be going wrong in your life right now. I know you never intended to end up in the condition you are in right now. This is why you need to build a relationship with the Holy Spirit so that He can help you live a comfortable life by changing your situation. As a matter of fact, ask God in Jesus' name to send Him, the Comforter, to help you right now. To comfort means "to console, relieve, ease, and make one feel relaxed." As I looked up that word relief it means "to liberate." The Holy Spirit wants to set you totally free from that addiction that has been causing you to be uncomfortable.

It can be very painful and depressing when you end up with an addiction, and it appears that no matter what you try to do to stop, the habit only seems to get worse. The Holy Spirit has a special way of letting us know that in spite of how bad we have messed up our lives, everything is going to be all right, a change is going to come, and God still loves us. Oh what a Comforter He, the Holy Spirit, is.

Let's also look at the second clause in verse 16, where it says that the Holy Spirit may abide with us forever. Once we invite Him in, He will come in to help us, teach us, lead, guide, and encourage us. He wants us to allow Him to assist us with cleaning our temple (life) up, and it doesn't matter to Him how long it will take. He will be right there. Our body is the temple of the Holy Ghost, not the temple for the devil and his demons to live in. Every demon that we allow to live on the inside of us is trespassing, and the Holy Spirit wants to teach us how to cast them out of us. To cast out means "to throw out"! He not only wants to teach us how to cast demons out of ourselves, but He also wants to teach us how to cast the devil out of others. Read **PIGS IN THE PARLOR** by **FRANK and IDA MAE HAMMOND**. This book will provoke you to do all that you can to make sure that a demon is not able to reside on the inside of you. When I first got saved I ended up wasting a lot of money on books, because I did not know which books to buy or which books not to buy. You have an advantage here, because every book that I am suggesting for you to read will be an awesome blessing in your life.

> *Luke 4:23*
> *And he said unto them, Ye will surely say unto me this proverb, Physician, heal thyself: whatsoever we have heard done in Capernaum, do also here in thy country.*

> *Isaiah 52:2*
> *Shake thyself from the dust; arise, and sit down, O Jerusalem: loose thyself from the bands of thy neck, O captive daughter of Zion.*

> *1 Corinthians 6:19*
> *What? know ye not that your body is the temple of the Holy Ghost which is in you, which ye have of God, and ye are not your own?*

> *1 Corinthians 3:16–17 Know ye not that ye are the temple of God, and that the Spirit of God dwelleth in you?*

> *If any man defile the temple of God, him shall God destroy; for the temple of God is holy, which temple ye are.*

That word *defile* means "to corrupt or pollute something or damage the reputation of." We all know that the devil does a good job at trying to corrupt us, pollute us, and damage our reputation. Without permission from God, demons can only do to us what we allow them to do. The Lord has promised us that He has given us power over all of the power of the enemy, and nothing shall by any means hurt us.

Luke 10:19
Behold, I give unto you power to tread on serpents and scorpions, and over all the power of the enemy: and nothing shall by any means hurt you.

Therefore, the portion of the scripture in I Corinthians 3:17 that says "if any man defile the temple of God, him shall God destroy" is only for people who are not trying to grow, refusing to grow, and hypocrites. I want you to know that the Holy Spirit will stay there and work with you as long as you need Him to and as long as you mean business with Him. He will not destroy you because of any little mistake that you make. He realizes we are not perfect, but we should all be striving for perfection. His main goal is to help us, not hurt us. Don't allow anybody to ever make you feel unworthy of the grace that we have that causes the Lord to desire to continue to work with us over and over in spite of our faults.

In John 8:1–11 the scribes and the Pharisees brought a woman to Jesus that had fallen in adultery they wanted stoned. Jesus' response to them was you that are without sin cast the first stone and they all being convicted of their own conscience left out one by one beginning with the eldest. When people are young in the Lord and haven't been through anything, they can sometimes be so critical. But if they just keep on living, they are going to go through some things themselves. I believe the eldest left first because he had been around for a while and had been through some things that allowed him to know that he couldn't afford to throw a brick at anybody for a mistake that they had made. The Bible says they were all convicted by their own conscience. That means they began to remember some things they had done that caused them to feel convicted and unworthy to throw the stone.

The Holy Spirit does not condemn us; He only convicts, reproves, and corrects us. All some people do is point the finger at someone else's sins because they have a self-righteous spirit or "an accuser of the brother" spirit. They act as if they are living righteously by their own abilities; this is so far from the truth.

> *Jeremiah 13:23*
> *Can the Ethiopian change his skin, or the leopard his spots? then may ye also do good, that are accustomed to do evil.*

Just as we can't change the complexion of our skin, believe me we can't change ourselves. But as we pray and continue to ask the Lord to change us, grow us up, and mature us spiritually, He will do it. So many people who get free from their addiction begin to pray for the wrong things. This is why we need the Holy Spirit to make intercession for us.

In John 14:17 we see that the Scripture is telling us that the world does not even know the Holy Spirit. If you are not saved, nine times out of ten, you do not even know the Holy Spirit yet. When you know someone you know what he or she likes and what they dislike. Well, the Holy Spirit desires for us all to get to know Him. He not only wants to comfort us, but He wants to help us with every situation that is going on in our lives. In Romans 8:26, the Scripture tells us that another one of the Holy Spirit's attributes is to also "helpeth our infirmities." First, we need to focus on the fact that the Scripture says He *also* helps our infirmities, expressing that helping our infirmities is not all He does. So I would like to take this time to formally introduce the Holy Spirit to those of you who don't know Him at all. And those of you who know Him, it is my prayer that you will know Him in a greater way than you have known Him before reading this book. I would also like to encourage you to read **THE HOLY SPIRIT IN YOU** that is written by an author by the name of **DEREK PRINCE.** I had been saved for twenty-two years before I read this book, and it was after I read this book that I realized that I did not know the HOLY SPIRIT as well as I thought I did.

A lot of times we end up in ministries that tell us to only read our Bibles. I thank God for the ministry of **Apostle, John Eckhardt**, the Senior Pastor of Crusaders Ministry, who has always encouraged all of his members to read books by other Christian authors, although I personally think he is one of the greatest authors there is, especially where deliverance is concerned. Make sure you get his book called **PRAYERS THAT ROUT DEMONS**, because you are going to need as much ammunition as you can get once you are set free from whatever addiction you are struggling with. The reason is, the devil is never going to give up on trying to get you back in the shape you were originally in, but his main desire is to cause you to end up in worse shape. The Bible tells us in Luke 11:24 that once the unclean spirit is gone out of a man the devil comes back with seven more devils more wicked than himself, and if they are allowed to come back in that person's life, their state is worse than the first.

Because I believe a lot of my audience that is reading this

book may not know a lot of scriptures, I was led to show you where to find the scripture verse/s and sometimes write out the actual wording of the scripture verse so that you will have a steady flow as you read this book and not have to stop and look up every scripture that is quoted. It is very important for you to know sound doctrine, because the Bible says that in the last days people are not going to want to listen to sound doctrine. Instead, they are going to want to be around people who will not tell them the truth. The Scripture says they are going to turn their ears away from the truth. This tells us that they will be listening to another spirit beside the Holy Spirit, because the Holy Spirit is the Spirit of Truth. Be careful when you find yourself enjoying carnal messages that are not helping you grow or that are not lining up with the scriptures.

> *2 Timothy 4:3-4*
> *For the time will come when they will not endure sound doctrine; but after their own lusts shall they heap to themselves teachers, having itching ears;*
>
> *And they shall turn away their ears from the truth, and shall be turned unto fables.*

> *John 16:13*
> *Howbeit when he, the Spirit of truth, is come, he will guide you into all truth: for he shall not speak of himself; but whatsoever he shall hear, that shall he speak: and he will shew you things to come.*

Now let's go back to Romans 8:26, and let's deal with the fact that the Holy Ghost wants to help our infirmities. The word *help* is a powerful word, because we as human beings usually get caught up in different situations that cause us to need some type of help. To help means "to assist somebody, to advise somebody, to make things better for somebody, to wait on somebody, and to prevent something from happening to somebody." We have some people who feel that they do not need any help from anybody. A person who feels that they do not need any help from anybody is really in need of more help than they could ever imagine.

The devil has a greater hold on a person who feels they don't need any help from anyone than one who realizes that they need help. None of us have been called to be a one-man army. We all need help with any infirmity that we have. An infirmity is a weakness, a character flaw, a sickness, or a disability. We all know that an addiction is a weakness that causes flaws in our character. Speaking from my own experience, drugs disabled me from doing a lot of things that I desired to do and caused me to do a lot of sick things that I thought I would never do. I became very weak to drugs and ended up with a whole lot of character flaws and other addictions as well. I definitely needed help that could only come from the Holy Spirit due to how sick I had become.

Also in Romans 8:26 the Scripture "lets us know that we know not what to pray for as we ought: but the Spirit itself maketh intercession for us with groanings which cannot be uttered." This verse is saying that when we do not know what to pray for as we ought to know what to pray for, the Holy Spirit will pray for us in a language we will not be able to understand. Of course, we all know that a natural person cannot interpret a groan. *Cannot be uttered* means "cannot be expressed or articulated." Although there are times that the Holy Spirit will make intercessions for us, the Holy Spirit will also pray through us, for ourselves, and for others. Jesus' disciples asked Him to teach them how to pray. The Holy Spirit will teach us how to pray if we ask Him to.

John 14:26
But the Comforter, which is the Holy Ghost, whom the Father will send in my name, he shall teach you all things, and bring all things to your remembrance, whatsoever I have said unto you.

The Holy Spirit is our teacher and He will teach us all things. He will teach us how to stop being rebellious, how to stop using drugs, how to stop drinking alcohol, how to grow spiritually, how to get strong, how to please God, how to raise our children, how to fast, how to pray, how to submit to leadership, how to operate in the gifts of the Spirit, and anything else we need to know. I believe one of his main objectives is to teach us things about ourselves. We all have a blind side when it comes to ourselves, and the Holy Spirit will definitely show it to us. We are always in a bad place when we begin to think of ourselves more highly than we ought to think. Sometimes, I think we take the credit for some of the things that the Holy Spirit has done through us and for us. This will really cause us to think of ourselves more highly than we ought to think. The Bible says that it is even the Holy Spirit who brings all things back to our remembrance, so let's not try to take the credit.

Romans 12:3
For I say, through the grace given unto me, to every man that is among you, not to think of himself more highly than he ought to think; but to think soberly, according as God hath dealt to every man the measure of faith.

John 14:26
But the Comforter, which is the Holy Ghost,
whom the Father will send in my name, he shall
teach you all things, and bring all things to your
remembrance, whatsoever I have said unto you.

Now, let's go back to Romans 8:27, *"And he that searcheth the hearts knoweth what is the mind of the Spirit, because he maketh intercession for the saints according to the will of God."*

The Holy Spirit searches our hearts. That word *search* means "to examine or investigate." When you examine someone, you are usually looking to see what the sickness or problem is and what caused the sickness or problem to occur. An investigator investigates. I believe the investigator finds out who did what, when, how, and why. The Holy Spirit knows the good things in our hearts as well as the bad things that have entered our hearts. We don't even know our own hearts. Let's look at what the Scripture says about our heart.

Jeremiah 17:9
The heart is deceitful above all things, and desperately wicked: who can know it?

Romans 8:27 also says, ". . . but He also knows what the mind of the Spirit is concerning us." that means that He knows what the will of the Spirit is for our lives, what's in order, what's out of order in our lives, and how He is going to fix it. He knows these things because He makes intercession for us according to the will of God for our lives. Isn't that wonderful to know that the Holy Spirit knows how to pray for us so that our lives can get in alignment with our assignment that God has placed on every one of our lives.

Romans 8:28
And we know that all things work together for
good to them that love God, to them who are the
called according to his purpose.

It doesn't matter what shape we are in, because some of us are in worse shape than others when God gets ahold of our lives. It doesn't matter where we start, what matters is where we finish. The Bible even says the last shall be first and the first shall be last. I believe God gets excited when He has the opportunity to work on people that others have counted out. He specializes in special cases. He is a specialist. Some people just need a doctor, but some of us need a specialist. And because we are called according to His purpose, and not our own purpose, He is going to make sure that everything is going to work together for good for us who love Him. I know the devil was laughing real hard when he saw the captivity that he had many of us in. But I know he is crying now as the Lord is using us to expose the works of darkness. I believe there are some things that dumb devil never would have showed us if he knew we were going to be set free one day and have the ability to warn others of his subtle devices, plots, plans, and schemes. Once God saves us and He knows that He can trust us, He will send us on special apostolic assignments. In other words, He will send us to spy out what is going on in the enemy's camp and give us the ability to see how the devil is trying to take advantage of us and make a fool out of us and some of the saints.

In II Kings 6:8–18, Elisha was able to see and hear everything that the King of Syria was planning to do to the children of Israel. This is an example of our spiritual ears and eyes being opened, as we discussed earlier. When I see the devil trying to work someone over, I automatically warn that person. I feel this way; since the devil likes to attack me, I might as well pass the first lick and give him a reason to attack me. We must understand that spiritual warfare goes with the territory. Some people think once they get saved all of their troubles are going to be over. But I came to inform you that the fight has just got started, because before we got saved the devil was just whipping us. Now, because greater is Jesus who is on the inside of us than he that is in the world, and we have power over all of the power of the enemy, we should be whipping the devil. I love it when the Lord allows me to win battles against the devil and his cohorts, because they did a lot of horrible things to me when they had the upper hand. God wants to put a payback anointing on our lives. A payback anointing is an anointing to pay the devil back for everything he did to us when he had the ability to do it.

Romans 8:29
For whom he did foreknow, he also did predestinate to be conformed to the image of his Son, that he might be the firstborn among many brethren.

We must understand that God knew us before we were ever born. He knew us before our mother met our father. That is why He told Jeremiah before He formed him in the belly that He knew him. You were not a mistake, you were planned. I don't care if your mother tried to abort you; you were still not a mistake. If your natural father didn't claim you, you were still not a mistake. If you were adopted or grew up in an orphanage or a group home, you were not a mistake. God wanted you to be birthed into the earth because He has a destiny for you. God knew exactly why, when, where, and what time you were going to be born. Because the devil did all he could to try to prevent you from being born and being alive today, that should let you know it is only because God has a great work for you to do in the earth. You were predestined to be here for such a time as this. Even when Jesus was born, the devil sought to kill him. When Moses was born the devil sent out a decree to kill all the male children, because he knew that a great leader was getting ready to be birthed into the earth. You were fearfully and wonderfully made, but the devil got in there and messed up your life. He couldn't mess up your life permanently because now you have street sense and spiritual sense. God is going to use everything that the devil meant for evil in order to use you to help many people stay alive. This is why God said in His Word that all things work together for good for those who love Him. God will even give you back every second, minute, hour, day, and year that you wasted in darkness.

> *Joel 2:25*
> *And I will restore to you the years that the locust hath eaten, the cankerworm, and the caterpillar, and the palmerworm, my great army which I sent among you.*

God has predestinated you to be conformed to the image of His Son. That word *predestined* means "to foreordain events; preselect who will go to heaven." That word *conformed* means "to make similar." Because you are predestined to be conformed to the image of Jesus, know that Jesus is the Word of God that became flesh and dwelt among men. God is going to conform your life, so that in the midst of a dark world, you will be able to allow the Word of God to be manifested in your life. The Bible lets us know that the earnest expectations of the creatures are waiting on the manifestation of the sons of God. God told me that these are the days that His power is getting ready to be manifested on the earth as it never has before. Azusa Street is not going to have anything on what God is about to do through those that He is getting ready to pour a heavy anointing on in this hour.

Acts 2:19 tell us that in the last days God is going to pour out His Spirit upon all flesh. To pour means "to flow in large quantities or rain heavily." God said He is getting ready to drench some of us with His anointing. Are you ready?

Know that God only anoints us for service, to do a work for Him in the earth. God does not anoint us to lie around and do nothing. The anointing does not come upon us so that we can feel good. It comes upon us so that we can perform miracles in the earth that cannot be denied. This is the season that many of us need to read the book of Acts again. It is time for us as the church to measure ourselves by the Word of God. There is a new hunger and a new thirst that is going to come upon many of us to see the miracles of God released in the earth on another level. There is a new generation of believers that God is raising up that are going to believe like David believed. He said the same God who delivered him from the paws of the lion and the paws of the bear is also going to deliver him from this uncircumcised Philistine.

We must contend for the faith that was once delivered to the saints. This is not the season to allow the enemy to water us down; we have got to walk in the raw power of God. That is why I believe God is getting ready to set a lot of drug addicts and alcoholics free. They did not want any mix in their drugs or any water, orange juice, or pop in their alcohol. They wanted it raw, straight with no chaser, and this is the type of anointing they are going to want—the raw anointing. They are going to want to walk in the raw power of God. God said all we have to do is ask. I don't know about you, but I want to walk in the raw power of God. I want to see my footprints on the devil's head. The Bible said that our feet will bruise his head and that we are going to kick him so hard that it is going to bruise our heel. Have you ever hit somebody so hard that you hurt your own hand? Well, it is time for a showdown because it is about to go down. Be strong in the Lord and in the power of His might.

> *Romans 8:30*
> *Moreover whom he did predestinate, them he also called: and whom he called, them he also justified: and whom he justified, them he also glorified.*

Once God predestinates us, He calls us. When someone calls you, it is up to you whether you go to see what he or she wants or not. God gives us a choice on whether we answer Him or not, or whether we go see what He wants or not. The Bible says that He came unto His own and His own received Him not, but as many as received Him to them gave He them the power to become the sons of God (John 1:10–12). It is time out for turning a deaf ear when we know the Lord is calling us to go deeper in the things of Him. The Bible talks about in the last days people will have ears to hear and hear not and eyes to see and see not (Mark 8:18).

Don't allow this to be you. Be very attentive to what God is saying to you in this hour, and if you do not have the ability or strength to do whatever He is telling you to do, ask Him to help you and equip you with everything you need in order to fulfill your assignment. God said if we ask Him for bread, He won't give us a stone, and if we ask Him for a fish, He won't give us a serpent. God is going to give us exactly what we ask Him for, especially when it is in line with His will for our lives and for His kingdom. He is our Father, and we do not have to beg Him for anything. All we have to do is ask and receive. God says that if we who are evil know how to give good gifts to our children, how much more will He give the Holy Spirit to those who ask Him? Once God calls us He justifies us. To justify means "to make righteous." Our righteousness is in Christ. Righteousness is the ability to do things right. Psalms 23:3 says "that the Lord will lead us in the path of righteousness for his name's sake."

Once the Lord leads us in the path of righteousness, the enemy will no longer be able to lead us to the drug house, the liquor store, or anywhere else that is not pleasing to God. Another attribute of the Holy Spirit is that He will lead and guide us into all truth. We need the Holy Spirit to lead us. Many people have gotten caught up in different types of addictions because they were following the wrong people. Be not deceived, evil communication will always corrupt good manner (I Corinthians 15:33). Hosea 10:12 tells us that when we begin to seek the Lord, He will rain righteousness upon us. I believe that the righteous rain that the Lord rains upon us when we begin to seek Him cleanses us from every spirit of addiction. God said He is raising up trees of righteousness in this season and that we are going to be like trees planted by the river of water, and we shall bring forth our fruit in our season. Fruit in the Bible represents two things: (1) It represents our character. God said that we will be known by our fruit not by our gift because a tree is known by the fruit it bears, and (2) Fruit represents souls. John the Baptist said bring forth fruit meet for repentance. It is time for the true sons and daughters of

God to be manifested in the earth. The best message any of us will ever preach will be by the way we live our lives.

> *Matthew 12:33*
> *Either make the tree good, and his fruit good; or else make the tree corrupt, and his fruit corrupt: for the tree is known by his fruit.*

> *Matthew 3:8*
> *Bring forth therefore fruits meet for repentance:*

> *Psalm 1:3*
> *And he shall be like a tree planted by the rivers of water, that bringeth forth his fruit in his season; his leaf also shall not wither; and whatsoever he doeth shall prosper*

> *Isaiah 61:1–4*
> *The Spirit of the Lord God is upon me; because the Lord hath anointed me to preach good tidings unto the meek; he hath sent me to bind up the brokenhearted, to proclaim liberty to the captives, and the opening of the prison to them that are bound;*
>
> *To proclaim the acceptable year of the Lord, and the day of vengeance of our God; to comfort all that mourn;*
>
> *To appoint unto them that mourn in Zion, to give unto them beauty for ashes, the oil of joy for mourning, the garment of praise for the spirit of heaviness; that they might be called trees of righteousness, the planting of the Lord, that he might be glorified.*

And they shall build the old wastes, they shall raise up the former desolations, and they shall repair the waste cities, the desolations of many generations.

Romans 8:31
What shall we then say to these things? If God be for us, who can be against us?

Many of us know that because of the lifestyles that we were living due to our addictions, we should not even be alive today. But if God is for us who can be against us? God has been there all the time. He was on our side because He knew we were powerless over our situation. If the devil had his way, he would have killed many of us a long time ago. Just count the times that you have had an encounter with death, but God intervened on your behalf. God knows that who is forgiven much loves Him much. Be grateful and appreciate the Lord for allowing you to be alive today, for healing you when you were sick, preserving you when the devil tried to kill you, and for watching over you and protecting you.

The Bible tells us that Jesus healed ten lepers, and only one came back to say thank you. Jesus asked the one who came back to say thank you, where were the other nine that He had healed. Some people have been shot up and didn't even tell the Lord thank you for healing them. Some people have been sick unto death and did not tell the Lord thank you for healing them. We have so many things to be thankful for. Do not forget to tell the Lord thank you! I thank Him for waking me up in the morning. I thank Him for allowing me to be clothed in my right mind. I thank Him for the activities of my limbs. I thank Him for food on my table. I thank Him for a place to stay. Most of all I thank Him for saving me.

Romans 8:32
He that spared not his own Son, but delivered
him up for us all, how shall he not with him also
freely give us all things?

God didn't even spare His own Son's life, but freely gave Him so that we could be saved, healed, and delivered. Jesus was wounded for our transgressions, bruised for our iniquities, and the chastisement of our peace was upon Him and by His stripes we are healed. He paid a great price for our salvation. If Jesus had not got up on that cross, I would probably still be a drug addict today or either dead. The bible says that while we were yet sinners, Christ died for the ungodly.

Romans 8:33
Who shall lay anything to the charge of God's
elect? It is God that justifieth.

Regardless of what we have done in our past, nobody can lay anything to our charge because we are God's elect, and God has made us righteous. Satan is always trying to release some type of charges on us because he is the accuser of the brethren. But I John 2:1 lets us know that if we sin, we have an advocate with the Father, Jesus Christ the righteous. We are God's elect. That term *God's elect* means we were chosen by God. The Bible tells us many are called but few are chosen. God has imputed His righteousness unto us.

Romans 8:34
Who is he that condemneth? It is Christ that
died, yea rather, that is risen again, who is even
at the right hand of God, who also maketh
intercession for us.

Even if you make a mistake there is no condemnation to them who are in Christ Jesus that walk after the Spirit and not after the flesh. Another attribute of the Holy Spirit is that He reproves the world of its sin. He never condemns us, He always reproves us. To reprove means "to correct gently." Even as Christ died and rose, we can rise up from any situation that we are in. We were all spiritually dead. Thank God that Jesus is sitting at the right hand of the Father making intercession for us.

> *Romans 8:11*
> *But if the Spirit of him that raised up Jesus from the dead dwell in you, he that raised up Christ from the dead shall also quicken your mortal bodies by his Spirit that dwelleth in you.*

> *John 16:8*
> *And when he is come, he will reprove the world of sin, and of righteousness, and of judgment:*

> *Continuing with Romans 8:35–39*
> *Who shall separate us from the love of Christ? shall tribulation, or distress, or persecution, or famine, or nakedness, or peril, or sword?*

Regardless of what we go through, whether it be tribulations, distress, persecution, famine nakedness, peril, or sword, we cannot afford to allow anything to separate us from the love of Christ. Regardless of what type of tests, trials, or tribulations you go through, don't run back to the world, because the devil will always try to get us to move from our place of protection. We are much stronger than we think we are. That is why the Lord allows us to go through things that we feel are too hard for us to bare. The Bible tells us in I Corinthians 10:13 that "there is now therefore no temptation taken us but such as is common to man, but God will with the temptation make a way for our escape that we may be able to bare it." Always run to our Lord and Savior Jesus Christ because remember we always win in the end.

Romans 8:36
As it is written, For thy sake we are killed all the day long; we are accounted as sheep for the slaughter.

The devil is devising some type of way to kill us all day long. That is all he constantly thinks about. The Bible tells us that he, the devil, comes to kill, steal, and destroy. Although the devil has already counted us out, Jesus has counted us in. Jesus has the final say in our lives; whether we will live or die. King David told God that he would not be able to praise Him from the grave. Many of us cannot die yet because of the work that we still have left to do in the earth. Sometimes, I have heard Christians say they are ready to go on home to be with the Lord. Well, I am not ready to leave this earth yet. I love the new life that the Lord has given me in spite of all of the opposition I have encountered from the enemy. Believe me, I have been through some hard trials since I have been saved, but in spite of them all I am still here. The devil tried to kill me before I was born, when I wasn't saved and since I have been saved. We are truly accounted as sheep for the slaughter.

In the third chapter of the book of Daniel, King Nebuchadnezzar got mad, full of rage, and furious because Shadrach, Meshach, and Abednego would not bow down to his golden image, which represents money, and instructed his men to heat a furnace seven times hotter than it should have been heated, in order to throw Shadrach, Meshach, and

Abednego in it. The men who threw them in the furnace were dressed in coats and their hats in order to protect themselves from getting burned, but the fire killed them as they threw Shadrach, Meshach, and Abednego into the fire.

The Bible says when the king went to check on Shadrach, Meshach, and Abednego they were still alive, and he saw a fourth man in the fire that looked like the Son of God. When Nebuchadnezzar saw that they were still alive, he began to praise the Lord himself and sent out a decree that whoever spoke anything against our God would be cut in pieces, because he had never seen any God that could deliver like our God. The Bible also says that Shadrach, Meshach, and Abednego were promoted in Babylon. Whenever we pass a test, whenever we don't bow down and worship the enemy, promotion comes. Obedience is the highest form of worship.

This is the season that we must rebel against any and everything that the devil tries to convince us to do. When we rebel against the enemy, this causes him to be full of rage and furious, but we have got to know that whatever we go through, the Lord will be with us just as he was in the fire with Shadrach, Meshach, and Abednego. God said another reason the enemy was so full of rage and furious was because Shadrach, Meshach, and Abednego passed the money test, because the love of money is the root of all evil. No matter how furious the enemy gets, always remember that in Isaiah 43:2, God promised us that when we pass through the waters, He will be with us; and through the rivers, they shall not overflow us: when we walk through the fire, we shalt not be burned; neither shall the flame kindle upon us. Even in my addiction, all of the horrible things I went through, I believe I passed through the waters, the rivers and the fire but I am still here to tell my story because God had a plan.

Romans 8:37
Nay, in all these things we are more than
conquerors through him that loved us.

We are not just conquerors; we are more than conquerors
through Jesus who loved us. A conqueror is a victor not a
victim. We are victorious. We have the victory over every
obstacle and every demon that tries to stand in our way.

Romans 8:38–39
For I am persuaded, that neither death, nor life,
nor angels, nor principalities, nor powers, nor
things present, nor things to come,

Nor height, nor depth, nor any other creature,
shall be able to separate us from the love of God,
which is in Christ Jesus our Lord.

Always remember, don't let anything separate you from the
Love of God.

Jeremiah 51:20–24
Thou art my battle axe and weapons of war: for
with thee will I break in pieces the nations, and
with thee will I destroy kingdoms;

And with thee will I break in pieces the horse and
his rider; and with thee will I break in pieces the
chariot and his rider;

With thee also will I break in pieces man and
woman; and with thee will I break in pieces old
and young; and with thee will I break in pieces
the young man and the maid;

I will also break in pieces with thee the shepherd and his flock; and with thee will I break in pieces the husbandman and his yoke of oxen; and with thee will I break in pieces captains and rulers.

And I will render unto Babylon and to all the inhabitants of Chaldea all their evil that they have done in Zion in your sight, saith the Lord.

As we see in Jeremiah 51:20–24, God refers to us as His battle axe and weapons of war. We will never meet the requirements of being God's battle axe and weapons of war without the assistance of the Holy Spirit. This is why the devil uses false doctrine to try to persuade people that the Holy Spirit is not for today. God spoke to me and said a Christian without the Holy Spirit is like a gun without bullets, ineffective.

To be ineffective means "to be unproductive, useless, and feeble." This is why we are told in the book of Jude:

Jude 1:20
But ye, beloved, building up yourselves on your most holy faith, praying in the Holy Ghost,

As we begin to pray in the Holy Ghost, it is like building spiritual muscles. People go to the exercise gym so that they can build body muscles, and we need to do spiritual things to build spiritual muscles. As we pray in the Holy Ghost, this causes our holy faith to be built up.

Prayer is another spiritual weapon that we have that is very effective; this is why the enemy tries to keep us from praying. The emptiest service in the church is the prayer service. I have seen churches with thousands of people in their services on Sunday and only a handful of people in their prayer services. If we do not pray, nothing will happen. The Word of the Lord says whatever we bind on earth will be bound in heaven, and whatever we loose on earth will be loosed in heaven. There is an order to everything that the Lord does throughout the Bible, but as far as prayer is concerned, we bind first, then He binds. We loose first, then He looses. In other words, when we pray, we have the ability to stop things from happening, and we also have the ability to cause things to happen.

> *Matthew 16:19*
> *And I will give unto thee the keys of the kingdom of heaven: and whatsoever thou shalt bind on earth shall be bound in heaven: and whatsoever thou shalt loose on earth shall be loosed in heaven.*

> *Matthew 18:18*
> *Verily I say unto you, Whatsoever ye shall bind on earth shall be bound in heaven: and whatsoever ye shall loose on earth shall be loosed in heaven.*

This is why we must force ourselves to pray even when we do not feel like praying. Spiritual battles are won through prayer and intercession. Intercession is when prayers are released on behalf of others. We should not just pray for ourselves, but we should pray for our families, ministers, and all who are in authority,

> *Nehemiah 4:14*
> *And I looked, and rose up, and said unto the nobles, and to the rulers, and to the rest of the people, Be not ye afraid of them: remember the Lord, which is great and terrible, and fight for*

164

your brethren, your sons, and your daughters, your wives, and your houses.

1 Timothy 2:1–2 I
exhort therefore, that, first of all, supplications, prayers, intercessions, and giving of thanks, be made for all men;

For kings, and for all that are in authority; that we may lead a quiet and peaceable life in all godliness and honesty.

If we do not pray we will not lead a quiet and peaceable life in all godliness and honesty. We have to pray for peace, we have to pray to live godly, and we have to pray to be honest. The enemy really tries hard to fight us in these areas. We cannot even be godly unless we are honest. To be honest means to be truthful. When we are not honest and truthful, it causes all kind of chaos to take place in our lives. Truth is one of our defensive spiritual weapons. Truth is so important that the Scripture tells us to put on the belt of truth first.

Ephesians 6:11–18
Put on the whole armour of God, that ye may be able to stand against the wiles of the devil.

For we wrestle not against flesh and blood, but against principalities, against powers, against the rulers of the darkness of this world, against spiritual wickedness in high places.

Wherefore take unto you the whole armour of God, that ye may be able to withstand in the evil day, and having done all, to stand.

Stand therefore, having your loins girt about with truth, and having on the breastplate of righteousness;

And your feet shod with the preparation of the gospel of peace;

Above all, taking the shield of faith, wherewith ye shall be able to quench all the fiery darts of the wicked.

And take the helmet of salvation, and the sword of the Spirit, which is the word of God:

Praying always with all prayer and supplication in the Spirit, and watching thereunto with all perseverance and supplication for all saints;

Although all of our defensive and offensive weapons are important, in this passage of Scripture, pay close attention to the order that the Lord tells us to put on the armor of God. No soldier should ever go out to fight the enemy without his or her armor on.

If you were getting dressed in the natural, of course you wouldn't put your shoes on first. So many people want to preach, but they do not have a lifestyle to go with it. This leads to disaster every time. We should put on truth and righteousness before we put on our preaching shoes. There have been times that the Lord has used me to preach a message, and afterwards, it appeared that I was tested on every statement that the Lord used me to make. Many people are offended when certain messages are preached, but have you ever thought about the fact that when the Holy Spirit is preaching through the preacher, He is also preaching to the preacher.

Preaching is a spiritual weapon as well. The Scripture tells us that we can preach deliverance to the captives. This means that even while we are preaching, sometimes people are getting deliverance. One day while I was preaching, the Lord spoke to me and said, "Jackie, deliverance is on your tongue."

IN ORDER TO GET HELP
YOU MUST REALIZE
YOU HAVE A PROBLEM

Luke 15:11–32
And he said, A certain man had two sons:

And the younger of them said to his father, Father, give me the portion of goods that falleth to me. And he divided unto them his living.

And not many days after the younger son gathered all together, and took his journey into a far country, and there wasted his substance with riotous living.

And when he had spent all, there arose a mighty famine in that land; and he began to be in want.

And he went and joined himself to a citizen of that country; and he sent him into his fields to feed swine.

And he would fain have filled his belly with the husks that the swine did eat: and no man gave unto him.

And when he came to himself, he said, How many hired servants of my father's have bread enough and to spare, and I perish with hunger!

I will arise and go to my father, and will say unto him, Father, I have sinned against heaven, and before thee,

And am no more worthy to be called thy son: make me as one of thy hired servants.

And he arose, and came to his father. But when he was yet a great way off, his father saw him, and had compassion, and ran, and fell on his neck, and kissed him.

And the son said unto him, Father, I have sinned against heaven, and in thy sight, and am no more worthy to be called thy son.

But the father said to his servants, Bring forth the best robe, and put it on him; and put a ring on his hand, and shoes on his feet:

And bring hither the fatted calf, and kill it; and let us eat, and be merry:

For this my son was dead, and is alive again; he was lost, and is found. And they began to be merry.

Now his elder son was in the field: and as he came and drew nigh to the house, he heard music and dancing.

And he called one of the servants, and asked what these things meant.

And he said unto him, Thy brother is come; and thy father hath killed the fatted calf, because he hath received him safe and sound.

And he was angry, and would not go in: therefore came his father out, and intreated him.

And he answering said to his father, Lo, these many years do I serve thee, neither transgressed I at any time thy commandment: and yet thou never gavest me a kid, that I might make merry with my friends:

But as soon as this thy son was come, which hath devoured thy living with harlots, thou hast killed for him the fatted calf.

And he said unto him, Son, thou art ever with me, and all that I have is thine.

It was meet that we should make merry, and be glad: for this thy brother was dead, and is alive again; and was lost, and is found.

In order to get free from any addiction, we first have to come to our senses like the prodigal son came to himself in Luke 15:17 and realize that we have a problem. So many people are in denial of their present circumstances, and as long as people are in denial, they cannot get the help they need. Notice, it was not until after the prodigal son had wasted all his money with riotous living, and had become broke and hungry, that he finally came to himself. Some of us have to hit rock bottom due to riotous living before we come to ourselves. That word *riotous* means "uncontrolled, disorderly, lawless, or rebellious." Whatever habits the prodigal son had, whether it was alcoholism, drugs, gambling, or sex, his actions caused him to end up broke. Money runs out real fast when you do not have any restraints.

After ending up broke and hungry, the Bible says that he ended up joining himself to a citizen (a person) in that country who sent him into his field to feed the swine (pigs). Feeding the swine had to be the lowest job on the farm, especially for a Hebrew. When we end up broke, hungry, and pitiful, it appears that the person who decides to put up with us always has some type of arterial motive that causes them to allow us to be around them, such as using us to be the dishwasher, the baby sitter, the errand runner, or the flunky.

The prodigal son was so hungry that he even desired to eat the husk that the pigs were eating, and nobody would give him anything. This denotes that even the person who had sent him into his field to feed his swine would not even feed him or pay him enough to be able to buy himself a meal. That is how it is in the streets. Once you have spent all of your money on alcohol, drugs, gambling, sex, or whatever your vice might be, the majority of the people that you have shared your money and drugs with will not give you anything. They will not allow you to live with them, they will not feed you, and they will completely turn their backs on you. As a matter of fact, I have been in places where they will put you out as soon as you have spent your last dime because they want to make sure that if anyone else is in the drug den getting high, they won't give you any, because it will be less drugs for them.

Some of the people on drugs can be the most selfish, vindictive, meanest, wickedest people you ever want to meet in your life. The desire for drugs causes a person to open themselves up to a lot of demonic spirits. Drugs transform a person into someone that God never created them to be. Although this evil transformation takes place in a person's life, God is able to transform them back into the person that He originally desired for them to be. Luke 1:37 tells us that with God nothing shall be impossible. It is not impossible for God to transform you into a kind, sharing, and loving person no matter how bad the devil has corrupted you.

In this passage of Scripture, the prodigal son also appeared to be homeless. It sounds as if he was actually living with the hogs in their hog pen. Although it may seem cruel that nobody gave him anything, it was good that they didn't, because that caused him to come to the realization that he needed to go back to his father's house where even the servants were living better than he was. When the Lord has a better plan for your life, He will not allow you to get comfortable in the state that you are in. While it will appear that others are having fun and prospering in their mess, your life will always seem to be in despair and going downhill. It will appear that something bad is always happening to you because those that the Lord loves, he rebukes, chastens, and scourges (Hebrews 12:6).

David said that it was good that he was afflicted so that he would learn God's statutes (Psalms 119:71). That word *statues* means "God's ways, orders, laws, or rules." He also said that before he was afflicted, he had gone astray, but now he has kept the Word of the Lord (Psalms 119:67). When God allows us to be afflicted due to the choices we make in life, the majority of us will never go astray again.

The Bible says that the rod of correction will drive foolishness far away from a child (Proverbs 22:15). After we get beat down bad enough due to our addiction, we will be glad for that addiction to be driven far away from us. After times have become hard for us due to our addiction, Romans 8:28 tells us that all things work together for good for those who love God and are the called according to His purpose.

When the prodigal son came to himself, he began to think back on how good life had been at home before he had previously left. He began to think about all those good meals he had been missing while he was looking at the slop the hogs were eating. He remembered how kind his father was and how good he had even treated the slaves who were working for him at that time. He said to himself, "How many hired servants does my father have that not only have enough bread to eat but also some to spare, while I am lying here about to die from hunger."

The prodigal son also had a very repentant heart toward his father. He told his father that he had sinned against heaven and had sinned against him. He felt so bad because of how he had done his father that he said that he was going to tell his father that he was no longer worthy to be called his son, and that he wanted him to make him like one of the hired servants.

The prodigal son left home very prideful, asking for his portion of the money, as if he could handle it and knew what to do with it. It is not good to desire material things before you are ready for them, because all you will do is mess the money up. The prodigal son left home prideful, but he came back humble.

This had to be a very humbling experience for the prodigal son, to leave home with a lot of money and then have to walk a long distance back home, due to not having any money, dirty, stinking, and most likely smelling like the hogs, because there was no clean water to bathe in. To top things off, I am sure that the same people who saw him leave his father's house with all the money that his father had given him were right there watching him barely able to make it down the road from being broke, tired, depressed, hungry, and worn out because of the lifestyle he had chosen to live. His walk home also had to be long, because the Scripture distinctly says that once he had gotten the money his father had given him, he moved to a far country. Oh, how we sometimes forget the old friends, neighbors, and neighborhoods we came from after we get blessed. Don't ever forget where you have come from. Stay humble, because if you begin to get prideful, you just might have to go back to the place you moved from for a while, because the Bible tells us that pride goeth before destruction and a haughty spirit before a fall (Proverbs 16:18).

In spite of the pride and all the bad choices that the prodigal son had made, when his father saw him walking down the road, he was so happy to see him that he didn't think twice about all the money that he had given him before he left home. The father was so happy to see that his son was still alive. The Bible says that when the father saw his son a long way off, meaning that he still yet had a ways to go before he made it to the house, his father ran to meet him, felt sorry for him, fell on his neck, and kissed him profusely. He was so happy to see his son that he celebrated his coming home by giving him the best robe that he had, put a ring on his finger, shoes on his feet, killed the fattest calf that he had, cooked it, and told everybody to come and eat and be merry because his son who was dead was alive again and who had been lost was now found. We have to realize that God is excited when we come to our senses, realize that we have a problem, and that we need help that can only come from our Lord and Savior Jesus Christ.

You may have grown up in the church, and after you got a little older, you wanted to go out into the world to see if you were missing anything out there. Due to this decision, you may be like the prodigal son, in bad shape right now. But as you make your way back home to Jesus, He has a new anointing for you. The prodigal son's father gave him the *best* robe that he had. I believe this robe represents promotion, honor, a new level of authority, a new mantle, and a new anointing, because once we backslide we come back in a worse shape than we were in before. Due to the depth of darkness that we allowed ourselves to get involved in, the Lord knows that we are going to need a greater anointing in order to be able to fight off the demons that would try to tempt us in order to try to get us to go back to our past lifestyle. This anointing also gives us the ability to withstand the tricks, traps, and snares that the devil will be forming in order to try to get us back.

Notice again that the prodigal son's father told his servants to put a ring on his son's finger.

The ring that was put on his finger represents covenant. A covenant is a promise, agreement, or contract. God will never break covenant with us. A ring is a circle, which represents never ending. The Lord is married to the backslider, and He promised us that He will never leave us or forsake us. Always remember the Lord never leaves us, but we sometimes leave Him, just as the prodigal son left his father's house. The Word of God also says that He has graved us in the palm of His hand (Isaiah 49:16). That word *graved* means "engraved." The Lord has engraved us in the palm of His hand, and He will not allow anyone to pluck us out of His hand.

> *Hebrews 13:5*
> *Let your conversation be without covetousness; and be content with such things as ye have: for he hath said, I will never leave thee, nor forsake thee.*

> *John 10:27–29*
> *My sheep hear my voice, and I know them, and they follow me:*
>
> *And I give unto them eternal life; and they shall never perish, neither shall any man pluck them out of my hand.*
>
> *My Father, which gave them me, is greater than all; and no man is able to pluck them out of my Father's hand.*

The prodigal son's father told his servants to bring his son some shoes. Shoes represent a new ministry. When the prodigal son went out and wasted the money that his father gave him with harlots and riotous living, made it through the famine and suffered hunger, this gave him the ability to minister to others who were going through the same things that he had gone through. The prodigal son now has street sense and spiritual sense, which allows him to know more about how the enemy operates in the kingdom of darkness. The very fact that he was able to make it back home after all he had been through caused another level of honor and respect to be given to him. The new level of honor and respect that the prodigal son was receiving caused his elder brother to get jealous. He was enraged that their father had killed the fattest calf for his brother and had told everybody to eat drink and be merry because his son who was dead was alive again and who was lost is now found. The elder brother said to his father, "You mean after he has gone and spent your money with harlots you are celebrating. I never left and you never gave me a kid to make merry with my friends." The prodigal son's father knew it was a blessing for his son to be able to make it back home after being lost and backslidden. He told the eldest son, "Your brother who was dead is alive again and who was lost is found." This shows us that once a person backslides, they are spiritually dead again until they come back, humble themselves, and repent. After they come back home, humble themselves, and repent, they are spiritually alive again.

Eleven

DRUGS ARE A SICKNESS

Mark 2:16–17
And when the scribes and Pharisees saw him eat
with publicans and sinners, they said unto his
disciples, How is it that he eateth and drinketh
with publicans and sinners?

When Jesus heard it, he saith unto them, They
that are whole have no need of the physician, but
they that are sick: I came not to call the righteous,
but sinners to repentance.

Drugs are a very serious problem. Drugs are demonic
spirits. Demons are the cause of people ending up physically
and/or spiritually sick. Many sick people go to the hospital
if they realize they are sick in their bodies. People on drugs
usually admit themselves into a drug rehabilitation center.
The church is a spiritual hospital. This is why Matthew 10:8
tells us to **heal the sick**, cleanse the lepers, raise the dead,
cast out devils: freely ye have received, freely give. James
5:14 says that if there be any sick amongst us let us call for
the elders of the church. In addition, Mark 16:18 tells us that
we will lay hands on the sick and they shall recover. God is
calling the church to walk in maturity, and in order to do so,

we must contend for the faith that was once delivered to the saints (Jude 1:3). It is time for the church to take off the patient's coat and put on the doctor's coat because the earnest expectation of the creatures are waiting for the manifestation of the sons of God (Romans 8:19). God is the only one who can deliver a person from drugs, because drugs are demonic spirits that need to be cast out. One of the ways we can tell that drugs are a sickness is by thinking about all of the sick things that they cause people to do in order to get the drugs. When you steal from people who have been good to you, that is a sign of being sick. Drugs have caused some people to steal from their own parents. Drugs will also cause people to put themselves in life-threatening situations. For instance, drugs will cause us to be willing to take a chance on going anywhere with a stranger in order to get high, which could cost us our very lives.

In addition, the majority of the time, we didn't know what we were smoking, snorting, or shooting. Many of us were so sick that if we found out that someone overdosed on some drugs, those were the drugs we wanted to find to get high off. I have had the opportunity during my years of being addicted to cocaine and heroin to even see people with pacemakers, severe asthma, and who were hooked up to oxygen machines sitting in drug dens smoking cocaine. Why, because drugs are spirits, and people are incapable of helping themselves. People need the Lord to help them. Once you are in this shape, you need a miracle! Many of us were so sick that we didn't even care anything about our future. We committed all types of crimes in order to get high that many of our criminal records ended up too bad for us to even get a decent job.

The way you know you are really sick is when you begin to

share needles with people that you do not have an inkling about what is going on in their bodies. You don't know if they have HIV, AIDS, or Hepatitis, but you are still willing to share their needle in order to get those drugs in your veins. All sick people are in need of a physician, and His name is Jesus. The prodigal son's condition was so bad that his father didn't even call him sick. He said he was dead and is alive again, lost and now found. Also, most drug addicts will end up lying anywhere. I don't know if the prodigal son was on drugs, but I do know that he was sick enough to lie in the field with the hogs and desiring to take a chance on eating the husks the hogs were eating. There is no hospital that can give you anything to stop you from getting high. This is a case for Jesus. Even people who go to the methadone clinic that have heroin habits usually go in order to keep from being dope sick, but they usually still snort or shoot heroin in addition to taking the methadone. Within the years that crack cocaine has been on the scene, there is still not a cure for crack cocaine. The only cure I know is deliverance in the name of Jesus! Drugs will also stop you from keeping your appearance up. Most drug addicts will prefer a bag of drugs instead of getting their hair done, a pair of shoes, a new outfit, or even a bite to eat because drugs are a sickness.

Twelve

ADDICTIVE BEHAVIORS

---

1 Corinthians 16:15
I beseech you, brethren, (ye know the house of
Stephanas, that it is the firstfruits of Achaia, and
that they have addicted themselves to the ministry
of the saints,)

There are many things people can get addicted to; some addictions are good and some are bad. As we see in I Corinthians 16:15, the house of Stephanas was addicted to the ministry of the saints. We should get addicted to seeing other people delivered and set free by the power of God once God has set us free.

Drugs are very addictive, and they cause addictive behaviors. An **addictive behavior** is any activity, substance, object, or behavior that becomes the major focus of a person's life, resulting in a physical, mental, and/or social withdrawal from their normal day-to-day obligations. In other words, drugs can make a person care more about drugs than their spouse, their children, their job, their health, eating, and even paying their rent, etc. If you study Addiction Studies in college, the classes are called Mental Health and Substance Abuse Disorders. If you write a proposal in order to provide services for people who are battling addictions, the grants are usually called Mental Health and Substance Abuse grants. This alone allows us to know that mental health issues and substance abuse go together.

Drugs are a work of the devil, but Jesus came to destroy the works of the devil (I John 3:8). Jesus will not only deliver people from the drugs, He will also regulate their mind. In Psalms 23, David tells us that the Lord restoreth our souls. Our soul is our mind, will, and emotions. Our mind dictates what we think, our will is what we want, and our emotions are how we feel. Once our soul is restored, we begin to think soberly, our desires change, and the way we feel about things begin to change.

According to the National Institute on Drug Abuse, drug addiction is a brain disease. Although initial drug use might be voluntary, drugs of abuse have been shown to alter gene expression and brain circuitry, which in turn affects human behavior. Once addiction develops, these brain changes interfere with an individual's ability to make voluntary decisions, leading to compulsive drug craving, seeking, and use. The impact of addiction can be far reaching. Cardiovascular disease, stroke, cancer, HIV/AIDS, hepatitis, and lung disease can all be affected by drug abuse. Some of these effects occur when drugs are used at high doses or after prolonged use; however, some may occur after just one use.

According to the Gateway Foundation, drugs are chemicals. Different drugs, because of their chemical structures, can affect the body in different ways. In fact, some drugs can even change a person's body and brain in ways that last long after the person has stopped taking drugs, maybe even permanently. Depending on the drug, it can enter the human body in a number of ways, including injection, inhalation, and ingestion. The method of how it enters the body impacts on how the drug affects the person. For example: injection takes the drug directly into the blood stream, providing more immediate effects; while ingestion requires the drug to pass through the digestive system, delaying the effects. Most drugs directly or indirectly target the brain's reward system by flooding the circuit with dopamine. Dopamine is a neurotransmitter present in regions of the brain that regulate movement, emotion, cognition, motivation, and feelings of pleasure. When drugs enter the brain, they can actually change how the brain performs its jobs. These changes are what lead to compulsive drug use, the hallmark of addiction. More deaths, illnesses, and disabilities stem from substance abuse than from any other preventable health condition. Today, one in four deaths is attributable to illicit drug use. People who live with substance dependence have a higher risk of all bad outcomes, including unintentional injuries, accidents, risk of domestic violence, medical problems, and death.

The impact of drug abuse and dependence can be far-reaching, affecting almost every organ in the human body. Drug use can weaken the immune system, increasing susceptibility to infections, and cause cardiovascular conditions ranging from abnormal heart rate to heart attacks. Injected drugs can also lead to collapsed veins and infections of the blood vessels and heart valves. They can also cause nausea, vomiting, and abdominal pain. In addition, drugs can cause the liver to have to work harder, possibly causing significant damage or liver failure; cause seizures, stroke, and widespread brain damage that can impact all aspects of daily life by causing problems with memory, attention, and decision-making, including sustained mental confusion and permanent brain damage; produce global body changes such as breast development in men, dramatic fluctuations in appetite, and increases in body temperature, which may impact a variety of health conditions.

When I first got saved and delivered from drugs, I used to have to write myself notes and stick them on the mirror in the bathroom in order to remind myself what I had to do the next day. Due to the Lord being a healer and miracle worker and filling me with the Holy Ghost who brings all things back to our remembrance, I no longer have to depend on those notes I used to have to leave myself.

> *John 14:26*
> *But the Comforter, which is the Holy Ghost, whom the Father will send in my name, he shall teach you all things, and **bring all things to your remembrance**, whatsoever I have said unto you.*

It doesn't matter what type of effects drugs has had on a person's life, the Lord is able to bring complete restoration, healing, and deliverance.

I am now addicted to the ministry. Old things, behaviors and appetites have passed away and all things have become new. I now hunger and thirst after righteousness because the bible lets us know that those that hunger and thirst for righteousness shall be filled.

Thirteen

DRUG OVERDOSE
STATISTICS

It is very important for us to know what is going on statistically in our economy and in our everyday lives. Knowledge is power. The Bible even tells us to study to show ourselves approved a workman that needed not to be ashamed (II Timothy 2:15). Knowledge is actually what you know. There are too many people in the world who do not know whether their children, relatives, friends, or spouse are using drugs. There is a lot of information out here, especially on the Internet. We are without excuse if we do not know what is going on in our everyday lives. Some people do not even watch the news. As I was writing this book, the Lord told me to look at the statistics on how many people die due to drug overdose, and I found it amazing that overdose is the leading cause of death, and more people die from drug overdose than automobile accidents.

We must study in order to see the strategies that the enemy is using to try to cause people to be in bondage and/or die before their time, so that as intercessors we can destroy the works of the devil through intercession. As we study, the Holy Spirit will bring back to our remembrance the spirits we need to be targeting in this hour. Below you will find the statistics that I found through my research. This is the season that God wants to empower His people and fill us with knowledge.

According to The Center for Disease Control and Prevention, *Drug Overdose in the United States:*

Fact Sheet, Overview and Definitions:

Drug:
Any chemical compound used for the diagnosis or treatment of disease or injury, for the relief of pain, or for the feeling it causes. A drug is either a pharmaceutical (including both prescription and over-the-counter products) or illicit.

Overdose:
When a drug is eaten, inhaled, injected, or absorbed through the skin in excessive amounts and injures the body. Overdoses are either intentional or unintentional. If the person taking or giving a substance did not mean to cause harm, then it is unintentional.

Misuse or abuse:
The use of illicit or prescription or over-the-counter drugs in a manner other than as directed. Deaths from drug overdose have been rising steadily over the past two decades and have become the leading cause of injury death in the United States. Every day in the United States, 105 people die as a result of drug overdose, and another 6,748 are treated in emergency departments (ED) for the misuse or abuse of drugs. In addition, drugs cause nearly 9 out of 10 poisoning deaths.

The problem:
Drug overdose was the leading cause of injury death in 2010. Among people 25 to 64 years old, drug overdose

caused more deaths than motor vehicle traffic crashes. Drug overdose death rates have been rising steadily since 1992 with a 102% increase from 1999 to 2010 alone. In 2010, 30,006 (78%) of the 38,329 drug overdose deaths in the United States were unintentional, 5,298 (14%) of suicidal intent, and 2,963 (8%) were of undetermined intent. In 2011, drug misuse and abuse caused about 2.5 million emergency department (ED) visits. Of these, more than 1.4 million ED visits were related to pharmaceuticals. Between 2004 and 2005, an estimated 71,000 children (18 or younger) were seen in EDs each year because of medication overdose (excluding self-harm, abuse, and recreational drug use). Among children under age 6, pharmaceuticals account for about 40% of all exposures reported to poison centers.

Most common Drugs involved in overdoses:
In 2010, of the 38,329 drug overdose deaths in the United States, 22,134 (60%) were related to pharmaceuticals. Of the 22,134 deaths relating to prescription drug overdose in 2010, 16,652 (75%) involved opioid analgesics (also called opioid pain relievers or prescription painkillers), and 6,497 (30%) involved benzodiazepines. In 2011, about 1.4 million ED visits involved the nonmedical use of pharmaceuticals. Among those ED visits, 501,207 visits were related to antianxiety and insomnia medications, and 420,040 visits were related to opioid analgesics. Benzodiazepines are frequently found among people treated in EDs for misusing or abusing drugs. People who died of drug overdoses often had a combination of benzodiazepines and opioid analgesics in their bodies. In the United States, prescription opioid abuse costs were about $55.7 billion in 2007. Of this amount, 46% was attributable to workplace costs (e.g., lost productivity), 45% to healthcare costs (e.g., abuse treatment), and 9% to criminal justice costs. Between 1998–2002, people who abused opioid analgesics cost insurers $14,054

more than the average patient. 400% deaths from prescription painkiller overdoses among women have increased more than 400% compared to 265% among men.

Among those who died from drug overdose in 2010: Men were nearly twice as likely as women to die; American Indians/Alaska Natives had the highest death rate, followed by whites and then blacks; The highest death rates were among people 45-49 years of age; and the lowest death rates were among children less than 15 years old because they do not abuse drugs as frequently as older people.

Among people who misused or abused drugs and received treatment in emergency departments in 2011: 56% were males; 82% were people 21 or older.

How Long Drugs Stay In Your System

Alcohol: 3–5 days in urine, up to 90 days in hair, and around 10–12 hours in your blood.

Amphetamines: 1–3 days in urine, up to 90 days in hair, and around 12 hours in your blood.

Barbiturates: 2–4 days in urine, up to 90 days in hair, and 1–2 days in your blood.

Benzodiazepine: 3–6 weeks in urine, up to 90 days in hair, and 2–3 days in your blood.

Cannabis: 7–30 days in urine, up to 90 days in hair, two weeks in your blood.

Cocaine: 3–4 days in urine, up to 90 days in hair, 1–2 days in your blood.

Codeine: 1 day in urine, up to 90 days in hair, 12 hours in your blood.

Heroin: 3–4 days in urine, up to 90 days in hair, up to 12 hours in your blood.

LSD: 1–3 days in urine, up to 3 days in hair, 2–3 hours in your blood.

MDMA (ecstasy): 3–4 days in urine, up to 90 days in hair, and 1–2 days in your blood.

Methamphetamine (crystal meth): 3–6 days in urine, up to 90 days in hair, 24–72 hours in your blood.

Methadone: 3–4 days in urine, up to 90 days in hair, 24–36 hours in your blood.

Morphine: 2–3 days in urine, up to 90 days in hair, 6–8 hours in your blood.

~Fourteen~

CONFESS YOUR SINS

---

1 John 1:9
If we confess our sins, he is faithful and just to
forgive us our sins, and to cleanse us from all
unrighteousness.

It is a sin when we abuse our bodies with drugs and alcohol. The Word of the Lord tells us not to be drunk with wine, which is excess, but to be filled with the Spirit (Ephesians 5:18). Now that we know we have sinned, it is time for us to confess our sins. Once we begin to confess our sins, God will cleanse us of all unrighteousness. We know that drugs are an unrighteous spirit, and it causes us to do other unrighteous things in order to get them. This is the time we can examine ourselves, confess, and repent of those things that we have done while we were under the influence of drugs.

God already knows that drugs are a mind-altering spirit and that we were not in our right mind when we did some of the things we did. God is very merciful, and although He already knows the things that we have done He still desires to hear us confess them. The Bible also tells us that if we cover our sins, we will not prosper, but whosoever confess and forsakes them shall have mercy (Proverbs 28:13). To prosper means "to grow, flourish or succeed." We will never succeed in life if we don't confess our sins. There is nothing that you have done that is so horrible that God will not forgive you. God loves us so much and He is very understanding. He knows how to separate us from the demonic spirits that may have possessed us or taken control over our lives and caused us to do certain things that we never would have done if we had not been under the influence of drugs.

Jesus is the Word that became flesh and dwelt amongst us (John 1:14), and the Bible tells us in Hebrews 4:12: "For the word of God is quick, and powerful, and sharper than any two-edged sword, piercing even to the dividing asunder of soul and spirit, and of the joints and marrow, and is a discerner of the thoughts and intents of the heart." God knows that we never intended to do some of the things that we did and stands ready to forgive us. Acts 3:19 tells us to: "Repent ye therefore, and be converted, that your sins may be blotted out, when the times of refreshing shall come from the presence of the Lord." We all need to repent so that our sins can be blotted out. Once you have been addicted with the spirit of drugs for a long period of time, you are probably possessed by a devil. Don't allow that statement to make you afraid. I must say this because the Bible tells us that we shall know the truth and the truth shall make us free. However, I was possessed by a lot of devils due to my drug addiction, but I am totally free today. Matthew 8:16 says: "When the even was come, they brought unto him many that were possessed with devils: and he cast out the spirits with his word, and healed all that were sick."

I have shared about my personal experiences and life as a drug addict in this book because I want everybody to know that if the Lord helped me, He can certainly help you. Don't try to hide anything you have done from the Lord. He knows everything about us anyway. Psalm 32:5 says: "I acknowledge my sin unto thee, and mine iniquity have I not hid. I said, I will confess my transgressions unto the Lord; and thou forgavest the iniquity of my sin." God wants to show us some mercy for the things that we have done. Mercy is when God does not give us what we rightfully deserve for the sins that we have committed. That is why it is so important for us to confess our sins. Proverbs 28:13 says: "He that covereth his sins shall not prosper: but whoso confesseth and forsaketh them shall have mercy." We can never prosper with a drug addiction. In addition, after we have confessed our sins and have forsaken them, the Scripture lets us know we will have mercy.

CRY OUT TO THE LORD
FOR DELIVERANCE

Psalm 34:6
This poor man cried, and the Lord heard him,
and saved him out of all his troubles.

The Lord cannot stand to hear us cry. Throughout the entire Bible we find that when people would begin to cry out to God due to various situations they ended up in, God always came to their rescue. Exodus 2:23-24 says that when the children of Israel began to cry out to God because of their bondage, God remembered the covenant that He had made with Abraham, Isaac and Jacob. A covenant is a promise. You don't know what God might have promised one of your loved ones concerning your life. When people begin to pray and cry out to the Lord, He begins to make them promises, and He is not a man that He should lie, neither is He the son of Man that He should repent; if He has made a promise He will surely bring it to pass (Numbers 23:19).

In Exodus 3:7, the Lord said, "I have surely seen the affliction of my people which are in Egypt, and have heard their cry by reason of their taskmasters; for I know their sorrows." A taskmaster is a person who puts a harsh workload on someone. Whenever a person gets addicted to drugs, the devil assigns demons, taskmasters, over that person to make their life hard. They have to do harsh things that they thought they never would have done in order to get high. He will take your pride and integrity from you, which will cause you to bend down so low that you would do just about anything. Almost all constraints and boundaries are destroyed at that point. People end up doing some things that are far too embarrassing to tell. Everyone, I don't care who they are, has had some skeletons in their closet. Everybody has done something that they are not proud of and refuse to tell anyone, whether they have been on drugs are not. Although there have been a lot of things that I shared in this book in order to help someone else get set free, I will honestly tell you that there are some things I would never share. The Bible even tells us that it is a shame to talk about the things that are done in secret by those that are walking in darkness (Ephesians 5:11–12).

Genesis 18:20 said that the cry of Sodom and Gomorrah was great and their sin was very grievous. There are a lot of grievous things that go on in the lives of people who are battling addictions. I have seen and heard about a lot of things that even grieved me when I was in my addiction. Although I crossed a lot of boundaries, I thank the Lord that there were still a lot of things He did not allow me to do, because now I know that there is a spirit attached to everything we do. I know people who are in church still struggling with spirits that they wish they had never listened to or bowed down to. These spirits are called strongholds. A stronghold is a fenced in or fortified place. Although a stronghold is a fenced in or fortified place, Jesus is able to break through every barrier. No matter what type of resistance the devil tries to set up, he cannot stop the Lord from breaking through. Micah 2:13 tells us that the breaker is come up before them: they have broken up, and have passed through the gate, and are gone out by it: and their king shall pass before them, and the Lord on the head of them. Jesus is the breaker.

Exodus 22:23 says that if demons afflict them in any wise, and they cry at all unto me, I will surely hear their cry; We have got to know that when we cry out to the Lord because of our afflictions God will hear our cry. When God hears our cry, he can't stand to hear us cry, so He will make the demons that are making us cry leave us alone so that we can stop crying. Drugs are definitely an affliction, and demons enjoy afflicting us because they love pain, darkness, filth, sickness, spirits of insanity, and poverty.

~Sixteen~

MAINTAINING YOUR DELIVERANCE

Titus 3:8
This is a faithful saying, and these things I will
that thou affirm constantly, that they which have
believed in God might be careful to maintain
good works. These things are good and profitable
unto men.

After God has set you free, do all that you can to maintain good works. Remember we are laborers with God and co-laborers with Christ. There is a part that we have to play. In Titus 3:8, Paul is speaking to his spiritual son, Titus, who was sent to set things in order as he ministered in Crete. One of the prophets said the Cretan people were liars, slow bellies and evil beast. Due to the lifestyles of the Cretans, Paul told Titus to rebuke them sharply, so that they may be sound in the faith. Some people have to be corrected in certain areas of their lives with the spirit of gentleness as soon as spirits manifest. That way they can be open to receive the deliverance that they need, so that they can be sound in the faith and grow up properly. Otherwise, they will grow up calling good evil and evil good.

If a person begins to call good evil and evil good, they will then end up having eyes to see and see not, and ears to hear and hear not, which will then result in their conscience being seared with a hot iron. Once a person's conscience is seared with a hot iron, they will no longer have a conviction when they do wrong things.

One of the attributes of the Holy Ghost is to convict the world of its sins. To convict means "to show somebody his or her faults." Therefore, in order to lay a strong foundation on the inside of people who come from certain realms of darkness, their spiritual ground has to be plowed. A plow is a tool (or machine) used in farming to loosen or turn the soil for initial preparation of soil for sowing seed or planting. I believe that Apostles and Prophets are plows, (instruments) used by God to plow and cultivate the soil of the hearts of people who have touched certain realms of darkness. The majority of people who have dabbled with drugs usually end up with a stony or hardened heart. If the Word of God is planted on a hardened heart or one that has not been ploughed, tilled or cultivated, the Bible tells us that they will receive the Word with gladness, but they will only endure for a while.

The books of Matthew, Mark, and Luke talk about the different types of soil (hearts) that the Word is sown on, but I like the example that is given in the fourth chapter of the book of Mark better. During plowing, tilling, or cultivation, the ground has to also have all of the thorns removed out of it, or else the cares of this world, the deceitfulness of riches, and the lust of other things will choke the Word, and that person will be unfruitful. Once a person's ground (heart) has been properly ploughed, tilled, and cultivated, the ground is good and they can bring forth fruit thirty, sixty, and hundred fold. The Lord prunes us so that we can bring forth more fruit. This is why the Bible tells us to either make the tree evil and its fruit evil or make the tree good and its fruit good. Evil trees are cast in the fire to be burned, and good trees are pruned. The good fruit that has had the ability to grow in our lives has to be maintained. This is why Titus 3:8 tells us to be careful to maintain good works. That word *careful* means "to be watchful, alert, vigilant, and cautious." To maintain means "to keep in an existing state (as of repair, efficiency, or validity): preserve from failure." In order for us to maintain good works, we have to sow to the Spirit by fasting, praying, reading the Word of the Lord, praising and worshiping the Lord consistently so that we will not fulfill the lust of the flesh.

We will not have good works in every area of our lives over night, but we must make sure that the areas that God has perfected are maintained. Always remember that the lepers were healed as they went. As you continue to follow after the things of the Lord, you will continue to be healed, set free, and delivered. Maintain your walk in the Lord, maintain your salvation, maintain your prayer life, maintain your fasting life, and maintain good works.

If God saved me He can save anybody! Please remember that my life was a mess, as I was trying to make it in the world that I once thought was a lot of fun, as I continued to fight against the original plan that God had ordained for my life. I started smoking cigarettes and drinking alcohol, at an early age, (age twelve). The spirit of addiction began to speedily take over my life, and before it was all over, I had turned out to be a hardcore drug addict. I was powerless and in captivity, but I didn't even know it. I was spending each day of my life using to live and living to use.

The church people would often stop me and try to witness to me before bad became worse, but of course, I refused to listen to them. Not to mention, I grew up living in the house with my grandmother who was saved, sanctified, and filled with the Holy Ghost. I was young, beautiful, and having fun, I thought. Of course that early in life, I didn't realize it was the devil telling me that I was too young and too cute to be saved, and that I would end up missing out on all of the fun that I appeared to be having at that time. I thought those thoughts were my own. Let's face it; Satan gets the majority of his work accomplished by causing many of us to believe that he doesn't exist.

The fun that I thought I was having drastically turned into a nightmare. My looks were gradually leaving me, due to my drug abuse. I had gone from drinking alcohol to smoking reefer, from smoking reefer to smoking angel dust and popping pills, smoking angel dust and popping pills to snorting cocaine, snorting cocaine to smoking cocaine, smoking cocaine to smoking cocaine and snorting heroin, and from snorting heroin and smoking cocaine to becoming an intravenous drug user. I was shooting up heroin and cocaine, speed balling, and smoking the cocaine pipe every day until I would literally pass out. It appeared as if I was playing Russian roulette with my life. I can't even begin to count all of the times I had an encounter with death, due to the reckless life I was living. However, in spite of my rebellion, God still watched over me and never changed the plans that He had for my life. Due to God's love and mercy, I am now living the life He has ordained for me to live. My life is now full of joy and peace. On January 24, 1992, I received a visitation from the Holy Spirit in the house that I was living in, and I was immediately set free. Yes, every drug demon that was holding me captive was cast out of me that day, and I have been delivered from drugs now for over twenty-four years.

Work out your own salvation with fear and trembling.

Pray: because men ought to always pray and not faint.

Fast: because it looses the bands of the wicked one.

Read the Word of the Lord: because it is your spiritual food and a weapon.

Praise the Lord: because the Lord dwells in the praises of His people.

Worship the Lord: because He deserves the glory and the honor.

Forsake not to assemble yourselves amongst the saints.

Obey those that have rule over you: for they watch for your souls.

Maintain good works: so that you will be steadfast, unmovable, always abounding in the things of the Lord!

The Bible lets us know in John 3:3 that we must be born again in order to enter the kingdom of God. If you have not been born again, ask the Lord to come into your life right now and give you a born-again experience so that you will have the ability to walk in the Spirit and not fulfill the lust of the flesh. It is my prayer that your understanding will be enlightened, and that you will realize that drugs are unclean spirits that have to be cast out of our lives and that you will submit to deliverance.

I pray that the strength of the Lord will be upon you to submit to God and resist the devil so that he will flee.

Father God,
I pray in the name of Jesus that you will deliver every
person who is reading this book from every demonic spirit
and stronghold that is holding them captive now. I take
authority over spirits of nicotine, alcohol, marijuana,
Sherman sticks, angel dust, cocaine, rock cocaine, heroin,
narcotics, prescription drugs, codeine, morphine,
methadone, and intravenous drug use.

Spirits of mind control, mind-binding, and mind-altering
spirits, I command you to go now in the name of Jesus.
Spirits of insanity, mental illness, bipolar, schizophrenia,
suicide, and depression, go in the name of Jesus. I take
authority over every spirit of perversion, illicit sex,
promiscuity, adultery, and fornication. I break all ungodly
soul ties off of their lives now.

I command every generational curse to be broken, and I
command spirits of rebellion, rejection, pride, and curiosity
to come up and out in the name of Jesus. I apostolically
decree that their minds will have the ability to comprehend
the deliverance that has taken place in their lives, and I
loose the consuming fire of the Lord to burn every fetter and
every chain attached to their lives so they can do your will
upon the earth. Strengthen them and cause the spirit of
holiness to rest strong upon their lives, and raise them up to
be those who will rule with the scepter of righteousness.

Make them bold as lions, and teach them how to walk in the
liberty wherewith you have set them free. Let their
discernment be keen, and give your angels charge over
them lest they dash their feet against a stone. Give him or
her the ability to see every trick, trap, and snare of the
enemy in the mighty name of Jesus!

YOU CAN MAKE IT